Bryan Sims is an experienced cc
leadership, and this book is a tour
Together takes on the huge and critical issue of organizational leadership development, including the ability to transform models of individual leadership to shared, collaborative, missional leadership. Offering a pathway to follow, this book is a gift to the larger church.
TOD BOLSINGER, AUTHOR, *CANOEING THE MOUNTAINS*

Bryan Sims not only shares his dynamic and inspiring experience as a kingdom leader but invites us to fundamental shifts that will challenge the status quo and release leaders to become catalytic change agents for kingdom movement. Jam-packed with spiritual theology, robust leadership practices, and game-changing strategies, this book should be required reading for anyone even thinking about leadership!
DANIELLE STRICKLAND, SPEAKER, AUTHOR, ENTREPRENEUR

In *Leading Together* pastor, professor, and author Bryan Sims makes a stellar addition to the leadership literature for those who are learning to lead off the map. He integrates missional theology, adaptive leadership, and the power of collaboration in a compelling and practical manner. Pastors and congregational leaders in the trenches, seminary professors, and future leaders will find this book exceptionally helpful. I commend *Leading Together* to you.
JIM HERRINGTON, AUTHOR, *THE LEADER'S JOURNEY*

In an era of highly disruptive change and the all-too-public moral failures of celebrity leaders in evangelicalism, we clearly need to reboot the system around more biblically resonant themes. For Bryan, kenosis, servanthood, perichoresis, and liminality are more than metaphors, they are doorways into an ancient-yet-new understanding of the leadership task. This outstanding book by my friend and colleague Bryan Sims could not be more timely!
ALAN HIRSCH, AWARD-WINNING AUTHOR ON MISSIONAL THEOLOGY, SPIRITUALITY, LEADERSHIP, AND ORGANIZATION; FOUNDER OF THE MOVEMENT LEADERS COLLECTIVE

The rise and fall of the solo-heroic leader has become an epidemic in the church. In *Leading Together*, Sims provides a remedy: The remedy is kenotic leadership—the humble descent of abiding in Christ, divesting of ego, and falling on our face before God. Reverse the trend and experience the kenotic fall and spirit-filled rise of shared leadership.

JR WOODWARD, NATIONAL DIRECTOR, THE V3 MOVEMENT; AUTHOR, *CREATING A MISSIONAL CULTURE*; CO-AUTHOR, *THE CHURCH AS MOVEMENT*

We all know it when we see it, and it takes our breath away. It's a highly functioning team of diverse men and women working together in a high-trust culture, accomplishing amazing results together. It is rare, but we have caught a glimpse of these teams in sports, education, music, and the church. How does this happen? In *Leading Together*, Bryan Sims walks us through Scripture and the best of leadership theory to give transferable principles that he illustrates with real people in real places.

JORGE ACEVEDO, LEAD PASTOR, GRACE CHURCH, SOUTH WEST FLORIDA

In *Leading Together*, Bryan Sims provides a timely framework for moving from solo-heroic leadership to a shared-leadership model. Sims recognizes that shared leadership isn't just a good idea; it's essential for transformation and multiplication in the church. What's more, Sims helps us understand that becoming mature leaders who share power begins with responding to God's love in our lives so that we learn to embody that love. This book will be a blessing for any current or future leader who desires long-term effectiveness for themselves and their team.

DR. ONEYA OKUWOBI, SOCIOLOGIST, RICE UNIVERSITY'S RELIGION AND PUBLIC LIFE PROGRAM; TEACHING PASTOR, 21ST CENTURY CHURCH, CINCINNATI, OH

Bryan Sims has written the book that every church leader needs right now. *Leading Together* avoids cookie-cutter advice and instead walks us down a path to understand the complexity of the current age and the way to move forward with clarity and power. If you feel stuck, tired, or even feel like throwing in the towel, read this book. It will open you up to new possibilities and the beautiful truth that you don't have to do it alone!

JACOB ARMSTRONG, FOUNDING PASTOR, PROVIDENCE CHURCH; AUTHOR, *THE NEW ADAPTERS* AND *BREAKING OPEN*

Finally, a team leadership book for today's challenges, full of disciplined research, personal experience, practical reality, spiritual enrichment, and melody for the heart. Bryan Sims deftly weaves his own life story, academic discoveries, scriptural wisdom, and years of coaching into the fabric of "oneness" Jesus prayed for us to have as his church in mission. The result is indeed the beauty of shared Christian leadership as holy harmony.

DR. RONALD K. CRANDALL, FORMER DEAN, E. STANLEY JONES SCHOOL OF WORLD MISSION AND EVANGELISM, ASBURY THEOLOGICAL SEMINARY, WILMORE, KY

The winds of change are blowing all around us. Many of the old ways of leading no longer work in today's complex and challenging world. One thing is for sure: the age of the lone-ranger paradigm of leadership is over. In *Leading Together*, Bryan Sims offers a biblical framework for shared leadership that reminds us that leading together is a means of grace empowered by the Holy Spirit. Read it, but most importantly, put it into practice with your team.

DR. WINFIELD BEVINS, DIRECTOR, CHURCH PLANTING, ASBURY THEOLOGICAL SEMINARY; AUTHOR, *MARKS OF A MOVEMENT*

Leading Together recovers a wholly Biblical vision of communal leadership that envisions the transformative power of the Holy Spirit as the primary agent of organizational and social transformation. This insightful text echoes the first picture of leadership in the Bible when Moses and the Israelites describe the leadership of God as one marked by redemption, empowered by unfailing love, and with the ultimate goal of holiness. *Leading Together* clears the way in the crowded field of leadership studies to recover an authentic Christ-centered approach to leadership.

CORNÉ J. BEKKER, DEAN AND PROFESSOR, THE REGENT UNIVERSITY SCHOOL OF DIVINITY

Bryan Sims is a gifted musician, sensitive leader, strong coach, effective teacher, and faithful Christ-follower. And in *Leading Together*, all these gifts converge to create a symphony of wisdom and a treasure of teaching. This is solid gold. Bryan leans on years of coaching for change to help us all sing a new song.

CAROLYN MOORE, FOUNDING PASTOR, MOSAIC CHURCH, EVANS, GA; AUTHOR, *ENCOUNTER JESUS*; *ENCOUNTER THE HOLY SPIRIT*; *ENCOUNTER THE FATHER*; *SUPERNATURAL*; AND *WHEN WOMEN LEAD* (FORTHCOMING)

History is *His* story—how good it is to know this in the VUCA-times we are in these days. It is crucial for God's children to know that he is in control and leads the way in working out his mission of hope. *Leading Together* inspires us to see that this is a joint venture in which we may discern the mind of Christ and act upon that as a community. Discover the privilege and the challenge of being co-workers of God in this thorough, lived out, and practical book!

JAAP KETELAAR, PASTOR, TRAINER, COACH; COORDINATOR, INTENTIONAL INTERIM MINISTRIES OF THE ALLIANCE OF BAPTIST & CAMA CHURCHES IN THE NETHERLANDS

Given the unprecedented challenges of our post-pandemic world, *Leading Together* is desperately needed today. Rooted in his profound immersion in Scripture and theology, his passionate, poured-out life as an all-in follower of Jesus, his several decades of fruitful ministry in leading and teaching others how to lead, his wide-ranging knowledge of leadership literature, and his rich experience as a musician and worship leader, Bryan Sims truly and beautifully shows us what spiritual leadership as shared leadership looks like. Here is a book that flows and overflows! You will be instructed and inspired as you read it.

STEPHEN SEAMANDS, AUTHOR; PROFESSOR EMERITUS OF CHRISTIAN DOCTRINE, ASBURY THEOLOGICAL SEMINARY, WILMORE, KY

LEADING TOGETHER

First published in 2022 by 100 Movements Publishing
www.100Mpublishing.com
Copyright © 2022 by Bryan D. Sims

www.100Mpublishing.com
www.movementleaderscollective.com
www.catalysechange.org

Cover image: Albert Beukhof/Shutterstock.com
Interior design and cover jacket design: Revo Creative Ltd

ISBN (print) 978-1-955142-12-0
ISBN (ebook) 978-1-955142-01-4

100 Movements Publishing
An imprint of Movement Leaders Collective
Cody, Wyoming

BRYAN D. SIMS

LEADING TOGETHER

THE HOLY POSSIBILITY OF HARMONY AND SYNERGY IN THE FACE OF CHANGE

100
MOVEMENTS
PUBLISHING

CONTENTS

FOREWORD

Unprecedented has become a ubiquitous word over the last few years to describe the volatile, uncertain, complex, and ambiguous (VUCA) times in which we are living. No doubt COVID-19 has accentuated these four characteristics across the world, but they were present long before the onset of a global pandemic. We live in a shifting culture, and the pace of change is accelerating rapidly. These radical shifts are stress-testing our systems, our spirituality, and our sanity. And so far, many of us are scoring a C-.

Our understanding of church, discipleship, and leadership is being challenged. The way we interact, learn, and listen is continuously adapting, and our minds, relationships, and institutions are struggling to keep up with this fast-paced change.

When the terrain is settled, known, and safe, we continue to use the vehicles and tools that have worked well in the past; the tried and tested strategies reign and rule. But when thrust into a world that is uncertain, unsettled, and constantly moving, we need to adapt, experiment, and innovate. The time is now, and we need each other more than ever.

On May 25, 1961, US President John F. Kennedy stood before a joint session of Congress and gave his Moon Shot speech, announcing that the United States would reach the Moon. The country would strive to do something that had never been done before. Clearly, they met their objective, but it took thousands of people to make it happen—men and women coming together, developing and testing prototypes and experiments, with cross-discipline teams working collaboratively to achieve the seemingly impossible. For those of us who are parents, this monumental effort is the equivalent of getting your kids out the door on a Sunday morning in time for church. Kennedy's words only became reality through the work of thousands of different people and a myriad of skill sets ... perhaps not quite the same as getting the kids out the door, but the point is, it's a team effort!

As Bryan unpacks in this book, there is no single personality, vehicle, or tool that will unilaterally allow us to adapt to an increasingly changing world. It is vital that we learn to listen to God and to each other. Differing perspectives, insight, and foresight help us to navigate these turbulent seas. No singular leader sees everything, every angle, or every scenario. We need to lead together.

Jesus was the archetypal leader. He also was the blueprint for a disciple-maker and a movement catalyst. As he initiated ministry, he identified a core team, lived in the context of community, listened to others, observed culture, spoke in story, and worked with and through others to release potential in individuals and wider communities. If anyone could've been a solo-heroic leader, it was Jesus. Yet he chose to lead with and through others. As we read the Gospels, we see the transition from followers, to disciples, to leaders, and finally movement makers. Simon Peter, the fisherman, really did become a fisher of people.

Sadly, too many churches nowadays have a single leader with multiple committees, a few disciples, and a handful of volunteers. It's as if we pick up our Bibles, and, instead of reading the truth of Jesus as a disciple-maker, we see him as doing everything single-handedly and leading alone.

As Bryan explores in these pages, Jesus epitomized the self-sacrificial way of leadership. He humbled himself, offering himself fully to others. He emptied himself in his relationships with his disciples and ultimately sacrificed himself on the cross for the sake of the world.[1] Jesus is the antithesis of our modern world of celebrity, title, and audience. He did not seek fame and fans but instead sought to follow his Father and make disciples. He calls us to walk in his way, not to lord it over others with title, power, or intellect, but to live and love as a servant.[2] In this book, Bryan implores us to lead, not as solo-heroic leaders who have all the answers, but as self-emptying leaders, who are willing to embody the selfless love of Christ and be humble enough to acknowledge that we don't have all the answers. We need God, and we need each other.

The picture painted by Bryan of a collaborative, discipleship-based, leader-developing, movement-making ministry reflects what we see in the life and leadership of Jesus. Bryan highlights a number of paradigm shifts we will need to embrace if we are to become the kind of collaborative leaders Christ is calling us to be in our contemporary culture. Be prepared to be challenged to move from command and control to equipping and mobilizing others, from intuition to intentionality, and from spectators and silos to participation and interdependence.

Letting go of our old paradigms won't be easy. But the solo-heroic leader, who single-handedly attempts to take on all endeavors, needs to become a thing of the past. As Bryan says, "Overcoming adaptive challenges requires shared leadership because no single leader is smart enough to figure everything out alone. None of us have enough intellect, experience, capacity, or resources by ourselves. Yet, as a senior pastor or leader, we often hold the false belief that the responsibility to make decisions lies with us alone." It's time to let go of those false beliefs, and as Bryan goes on to say, to become the kind of humble leaders who will admit that we can't solve problems alone, and to invite wise and Christlike people to lead with us. Throughout these pages, Bryan shows us that good leaders are cultural architects—leaders who create the culture in which transformation is possible.

For almost three decades Bryan has championed, embodied, and coached individuals and teams to engage with collaborative, shared leadership. His insight, wisdom, and experience can help us navigate the volatile, uncertain, complex, and ambiguous world we find ourselves in.

As part of Spiritual Leadership, Inc. (SLI), Bryan and his colleagues have been coaching churches and teams for more than two decades to deepen the Christlikeness of leaders and teams. They have a coaching process that marries both the spiritual and strategic, a hallmark of Bryan's life and this book.

Leading Together is written to the leader who wants to release potential in others. It is also written for those who no longer want to struggle alone. If you are weary and feel burnt out from the solo-heroic leader narrative, tired of having to have every answer for every question, then this book is for you. If you are longing for ministry to be collaborative and have a heart and hope to release kingdom potential in and through others, then join on this journey and allow the pages of this book to bring life to your dry bones.

Alan Hirsch and Rich Robinson

PRELUDE

In March 2020, a pandemic abruptly interrupted our lives. Little did we know how much would change and how many challenges would emerge—both in our lives and in our leadership. Though it can feel overwhelming, it is in seasons of disruption that the culture of the future is created.[1]

Many congregations, missional communities, denominations, and mission organizations have been dissatisfied with their impact and fruitfulness for some time, but the inertia of the status quo and the complexities of the challenges blind them to future possibilities. What if, in this season of disruption, the Holy Spirit could enable us to see with fresh eyes and move us in new directions?

Faced with this unprecedented opportunity, what kind of leaders must we be to see the church become all that God has called us to be in our generation? How can we discern and embody new patterns for making disciples and growing spiritual leaders? How can we equip and empower others in such a way that leading becomes a shared experience with multiplying impact? These are the questions that prompted this book.

It has always captivated my attention to imagine the contemporary church living and breathing the gospel as the early Christians did in the book of Acts. I dream of an equipped church that embodies the kingdom Jesus constantly demonstrated and discussed with his disciples. I picture the world knowing that Christians belong to Jesus because of how we authentically follow him and because of how we love one another.[2] I imagine the blurring of lines between those who are "professional" Christians and those who are not. I envision the body of Christ together in relationship and purpose, mature and representing the fullness of Jesus in the world.[3]

But do I believe God can actually change things? Is there really any possibility of seeing the kind of awakening and movement we saw in the book of Acts? If there is, what will it require of me? Of us? And can it happen now?

I think so.

As a boy, I lived in a tiny, insignificant town. Though I felt small, I couldn't quite shake the feeling that I must be made for something bigger. I remember intimate talks with my younger brother, when we would imagine *more*. I could see the passion in his eyes and hear the courage and trusting audacity in his voice as he declared, "Why not?" Even then, I believed God could do big things.

Over time, God began showing me how he could radically change people and situations.

As a child, I watched a group of Christians pray through tense theological and denominational division in a city, which eventually led to revival and unity. In college, I helped lead a group of students in passionate worship and fervent prayer for mission that transformed the culture of a campus. Jesus was exalted and the Spirit empowered young people to be Jesus' hands and feet throughout the world. As a young husband, my wife, MyLinda, and I watched as a random collection of young people became a unified mission team and saw many lives transformed, including our own. As a teacher and coach, I walked alongside countless leaders and teams of ordinary Jesus-followers who grew in unity and maturity and fruitfully impacted their places of influence.

In each of these contexts, the transformation came in the midst of significant challenge and disruption. The transformation was entirely God's work, but ordinary Jesus-followers were engaged and empowered to participate as the Spirit enabled.

As you think about your own context, be encouraged that God can bring transformation, no matter the challenges we face.

WHERE WE FIND OURSELVES

A look across the current landscape of the church in the West could easily discourage us. The historic church in Europe has lost its impact and influence, as generations of people practiced lifeless religion rather than engaging in authentic mission as disciples of Jesus, and post-Christian belief became the norm.[4] On a similar path, the church in North America is declining and largely ineffective. As evidence, we need look no further than the rising number of the "Nones"[5] as well as the negative perceptions of "outsiders."[6] Churches are closing at a rapid rate. Many Christians exhibit a lifestyle that is no different than their non-believing counterparts. Brokenness and addiction are rampant both inside and outside the church. Division, hate, emotional immaturity, and a complete erosion of our ability to engage in civil discourse are evident both in our society and within the church. This cannot possibly be the kind of church God has called us to be.

From years of research, along with experience coaching and leading in many church contexts, I see two major cultural shifts needed in many Christian organizations. The first is a shift from the *privilege and status of membership* in the church to a Jesus-movement ethos that equips and mobilizes ordinary disciples to *be the church*. For too long, we have been stuck in the paradigm of a consumeristic church culture—as if everything exists to serve the individual member. This leads to the professionalization of leaders who perform ministry tasks in a sort of buffet for consumers. While not likely intended, the consequence of this model is a culture of passive observation rather than active reception of grace and empowerment for mission. Ordinary Christians often end up feeling left out of the "real" mission and ministry, and they grow either complacent or resentful toward the church.

The second shift is from *solo leadership* to *shared leadership*. We've fallen into the trap of believing that only a lone senior leader can be the vision holder. Only s/he knows what is best for the organization they lead.[7] But is this "solo-heroic" form of leadership really the best model? Will it help us face and overcome our current challenges?

When we look at the example of Jesus, we see a leader with a team of disciples who eventually multiplied his impact. In contrast, our church leadership often tends to mirror celebrity culture, and as previously mentioned, our people function more like consumers of religious goods and services than active participants in the body of Christ. Data and experience demonstrate how dysfunctional such leadership can be and how often it is limited to single-generation impact.[8] In other words, the charisma of such a leader is not replicable or multipliable, and therefore cannot be repeated by those who follow them. Organizations under this type of leadership are worse off in the long run. In addition, our leaders have also typically been men, limiting the leadership perspective primarily to one gender, and in so doing inhibiting a healthier organization. Though this solo-heroic type of leadership has done much damage within church culture, it remains strong in our leadership muscle memory.

The challenges facing the church and much of today's world are often referred to as *adaptive challenges,* because they will require us to adapt or be transformed in order to overcome them.[9] The COVID-19 pandemic presented a very real adaptive challenge because we were faced with circumstances none of us had previously faced and none of us knew exactly how to lead through. Reaching young people with the gospel presents another adaptive challenge, given so few seem interested in church. Leaders often try to apply current know-how to face these challenges, but that seldom works, because what is actually required is for us to *change.*

Have you ever seen the breathtaking beauty of a flock of birds moving together in unison?[10] It is most common with starlings, and this movement together is referred to as a *murmuration.* It occurs when hundreds to thousands to even millions of birds look like one single mass in the sky. When a murmuration turns together in unison, it is an innovative and dynamic response to an external factor pushing against it.[11] In other words, when the birds face an adaptive challenge, they move together to adapt and survive as one imposing force rather than a collection of individuals.

While there are plenty of things the church knows how to do well, much of our current ineffectiveness is caused by us trying to solve problems individually and not having the skills or mindset required to overcome the adaptive challenges we face. Perhaps we should take our cue from the starlings. Instead, we often lack the skills to shift our paradigms and change our culture.

Where does this leave us?

OUR SURE HOPE

Is God good? Is Jesus still Lord? Are we still filled and empowered by the same Spirit that raised Christ from the dead? Is the kingdom of heaven still among us?

The answer to these questions is most certainly *yes*! While it may be that the Lord is grieved by much of the current reality, we can rest assured that the Triune God is not anxious or stressed about how to handle the challenges we face. The Spirit of God hovers over the chaos and has consistently transformed similar situations throughout history. God will prevail, and the gates of hell will not stand against his church.[12]

Above all, we know that God is not lacking creativity, and—to the surprise of many in the Western church—the *global* church is actually growing more rapidly now than ever before in history. God is moving in his world!

The church in Africa and Latin America is increasing rapidly—both through many people coming to Christ and through church-planting movements.[13] In Europe and in North America, there is encouraging multiplication of new churches and new expressions of church through movements and networks such as Fresh Expressions, V3, New Thing, and Forge.[14] Some denominations and associations of churches are also seeing significant renewal. As examples, see groups like the Anglican Church North America, the Christian & Missionary Alliance, Eco-Presbyterian, and New Room Network.[15] If this momentum continues, are we perhaps in the beginning stages of the next Great Awakening?

WHAT'S NEXT?

If we have sure hope in who God is and what he is doing in the world, what must happen next to close the gap between our current reality and the mature church we dream of? We need a different type of leadership. We need leaders who abide in Jesus; who empower each person to use their gifts; and who create teams that reflect the diversity we see in the kingdom of God. Such leaders discern and keep in step with the Spirit. They focus more on spiritual movements than on numbers of people and dollars collected. This type of leadership is necessary to truly embody movement DNA[16] and to face the adaptive challenges of today's world.

Though there is no silver bullet or easy answer, there *is* a pathway to transformation; but taking that pathway will require us to go *through* the challenges ahead. Our natural inclination is to avoid pain and difficulty; to bury our heads in the sand, and stay busy in our areas of technical expertise. Instead, we will have to learn to courageously walk forward on this journey, in step with and empowered by the Spirit of Christ, and *together* with other disciple-leaders.

MY JOURNEY

Over the past two decades, I have had the great privilege of walking alongside many leaders, teams, churches, and organizations as a coach with Spiritual Leadership, Inc. (SLI).[17] For the past ten years I have also helped to equip both emerging and experienced leaders as a professor at Asbury Theological Seminary.[18] While there are certainly many challenges facing the church today, I come to this point in my own journey deeply hopeful and encouraged with what God is doing in the world and the holy possibilities for the church in this generation. I shared some of my dreams earlier in this chapter, but I want to invite you further into my own story here.

I enjoy a number of hobbies, many of which have to do with sports and the outdoors; but one that has shaped me most and is deeply part of me involves music. I grew up in a musical home. My mom was a music teacher, and my dad, though an athletic coach by profession, was a vocalist and guitar player who sang in a soul band and eventually became the worship leader in my home church. Over time my whole family participated in that worship team. I eventually did an undergraduate degree in music, taught music in a Christian school, and started a band. Together, our band wrote and recorded music and traveled throughout our region, leading concerts, worship services, revivals, conferences, and church camps. While my own calling is not directly tied to music, I do believe the beauty of music can provide a powerful metaphor for shared leadership in the church. (We will return to this throughout the book.)

That little congregation where my family helped lead worship was a healthy non-denominational church where I was intentionally discipled in the way of Christ. The church honored God, was Christ centered, and sought to be led by the Spirit. The equipping I received from a young age occurred in an environment of grace that fostered the exploration and development of my own spiritual gifts and maturity. In fact, I was given opportunities to share in leadership and speak to the congregation as early as middle school and found myself playing bass guitar and singing in the worship team by early high school. Because of the culture of this church, I assumed it to be normative that the whole body of Christ was engaged, equipped, and mobilized.

As a young man, I sensed a particular calling to be a missionary to the university in my hometown—West Texas A&M. Along with a handful of diverse students from all sorts of Christian backgrounds, I had the honor of launching a college worship service on campus. We lifted high the name of Jesus Christ and saw hundreds of students dramatically impacted by the love of God they experienced in those services. The powerful sense of community that developed in those years propelled a number of my friends out around the globe as Christ's ambassadors. The hand of the Lord was upon us in remarkable ways.

Yet in the midst of that exciting ministry, I sensed a growing frustration. Students who were transformed by the love of God on those glorious mountain tops of worship had no *environment* or *process* to mature them in what God was seeking to do in their lives. At the same time, I was employed in a church plant that prioritized outreach and evangelism but had no corollary process whatsoever for discipling those who had been reached or for raising up spiritual leaders. (That church plant eventually folded.)

After a season of missionary work in Panama, MyLinda and I sensed the need for further equipping and deepening in the Lord. During that time two passages of Scripture gave perspective and motivation to the call before us. The first, a verse in Revelation, spoke to our hearts about our role as the bride of Christ: "Let us rejoice and exult and give him the glory, for the marriage of the Lamb has come, and his Bride has made herself ready" (Revelation 19:7 ESV).

As the church, we are Christ's bride. We cannot be the bride by ourselves. Only *together* with the whole body of the church can we be the bride of Christ. MyLinda and I felt an urgent need to pursue how we could become more readied to join others in being Jesus' faithful bride. In response to God's great love for us, we wanted to see the church become a bride that truly loves God and our neighbor. We wanted to walk in the way of discipleship as sold-out followers of Jesus. And we sensed the need to better equip the body of Christ to engage in God's mission of love to the world.

The second Scripture the Lord gave us was Ephesians 4:11–16, where Paul describes the diverse gifts Jesus gave to the church for the purpose of *equipping the saints for the work of ministry* that leads specifically to *unity* and *maturity* in the body of Christ. In this description, Paul paints the picture of the church being *the measure of the full stature of Christ* in the world where we grow up into Christlikeness as we are built up in love.

The Spirit of the Lord burned deep within us, particularly highlighting the themes of "equipping" and "unity." We asked ourselves this crucial question, "How can we grow into true maturity—even to the measure of the full stature of Christ?" And while it's easy to wonder if we can truly grow up in Christ, we felt that God would not have invited us to do so without making such growth possible.

This passion for equipping others in order to see unity and maturity in the bride of Christ would require a great deal of me. It did then, and it still does today. I've shared with you some of the amazing and transformative things I have been grateful to see and experience in my lifetime, and I give God the glory for it all. What I haven't yet shared is how broken and insecure I have been throughout much of that journey. I have grown to realize that if I want to see maturity in the body of Christ, I have to be willing for the Holy Spirit to do whatever it takes to bring maturity in *me*. God is gracious, patient, and full of mercy in that process, but it is still painful. I've had to confront my own self-orientation and pride that consistently puts myself over others even when I don't want it to be that way. I've had to admit that fear and control have often been present in my life and leadership rather than love and trust. These revelations often make me want to hide from others, but it is in relationship with others that I can find healing and growth as God works in me.

What I learned in this process is that God longs for us to become like Jesus—to *be* what Jesus modeled for us. And the Holy Spirit longs to mature and empower us within the body of Christ. I had to experience the Lord's love and mercy myself, and in response, to continually empty myself in deep surrender to the Lord and with others. This is where the well of deep joy resides, and the fruit of this over time is indeed maturity in Christ.

This maturing continued in me as the Lord led me to enroll in seminary. My passion deepened in this season, as did my relationship with God. As a student, I had the great honor to begin working as a leadership and congregational coach for SLI (a new organization at the time). SLI coaching was based on three generative principles:

1. becoming *spiritual leaders* in covenant community
2. *creating environments* that foster transformation
3. *developing processes* that bear fruit

These emphases on spiritual growth, team leadership, spiritual leadership development, and continual growth of fruitfulness in mission helped me to learn the importance of living in accountable relationships. Mutual covenant and loving questions regarding my daily walk with Jesus have helped me continue to mature and to discern God's will and ways with others.

Serving as a pastor in multiple denominations (non, Methodist, Baptist, Anglican), as an SLI coach, and as a seminary professor, I have interacted with many pastors and lay leaders who have a deep desire for growth but are ill-equipped to lead their congregations into the fruitfulness they long for. These leaders often lack the framework, character, environment, and processes necessary to move their congregations forward. Time and again they have lost sight of their first love and primary calling to abide in Jesus. For far too many—laity and clergy alike—ministry in the local church has degenerated to merely maintaining the status quo or trying to survive as an institution rather than making disciples who are embodying the kingdom of God and transforming the world. I have encountered many leaders who are frustrated, isolated, overwhelmed, burned out, feeling stuck in life and ministry, and questioning their call. But truly, one of my greatest joys has been to see some of these same leaders rediscover their primary call to abide in Christ's presence and then to be coached into effective leadership. My hope is that this book will enable more leaders to step into the fruitfulness that Christ has for them and the people they serve.

WHAT TO EXPECT

There are three major sections in this book.

In part one we will take a deep dive into why adopting a new paradigm of shared spiritual leadership is essential, both in terms of the realities we face, and in light of what we see in the nature of God and in Scripture.

Part two offers an exploration of the overall framework of shared spiritual leadership, with attention given first to God's role in our leadership and transformation. This is followed by a description of the big-picture pathway from your current reality, through a new paradigm of leadership, into a new transformed and transforming reality.

Having laid these foundations, part three will present the three key roles of spiritual leaders in this new paradigm and will point toward practices required to embody shared spiritual leadership together and experience fruitfulness.

All of this will be framed using the Gospels and the book of Acts and will be presented alongside modern-day stories of transformation where shared spiritual leadership is embodied.

THIS BOOK IS FOR YOU

Throughout this book, I will refer to many current case studies and stories from churches, both to illustrate the gravity of the adaptive challenges the church is facing today and the beauty of the transformative work of the Spirit through disciples embodying the harmony and synergy of shared spiritual leadership together.

I am writing to pastors who may feel stuck, burned out, and merely trying to survive. It is possible for you to have partners in this journey, and it is Jesus' desire that you experience his complete joy.

I am writing to missional leaders who have always imagined a kingdom-invaded world. Just because you are facing challenges you have not faced before doesn't mean you need to give up on the dream that God has planted in you.

I am also writing to Christian lay leaders who are feeling a tug (dare I say a calling) to be "all in" with Jesus, but who may not feel qualified to participate in his mission. You may even be imagining what it would look like to become a missionary to your workplace or how you can overcome the greatest adaptive challenges in your community. Know today that it is God's voice you are hearing, and he is inviting you to something deeper.

Finally, I am writing to denominational and network leaders who feel removed from the on-the-ground work and wonder what it looks like in this season to live the calling you have received. You may sense that your system needs an overhaul, but you don't feel like you have any idea how to lead it … or even participate in it. There is hope for you. The Spirit has always been and will always be in the business of bringing resurrection where there has been death.

AWAKEN YOUR DREAM

Whether you are already leading or you are an emerging leader, I want you to imagine the holy possibility of what your community can and will look like when the kingdom of God comes in your context. Begin to picture being on the other side of the greatest adaptive challenges you are currently facing and imagine who will have b een on that journey of shared spiritual leadership with you. As you begin reading, ask the Holy Spirit to give you (and your team) wisdom and discernment to follow Jesus through the unknown territory that lies ahead, and into a new reality that echoes the realities of God's kingdom.

Let's start the journey of leading together.

PART 1

WHY SHARED LEADERSHIP?

We begin this journey by looking at the paradigm of shared spiritual leadership. In the opening chapter, we will dive into two of the most dramatic adaptive challenges in the book of Acts and see how the early church leaders navigated them. In chapter two, we will look at the characteristics and consequences of solo-heroic leadership, and in chapter three, we contrast those with a biblical model for shared spiritual leadership.

1

LEARNING TO LISTEN: KENOSIS AND ADAPTIVE LEADERSHIP

I learned to read music early in life, working on whatever piece my piano teacher gave me; but my true love for music began in high school, with a longing to play jazz. At age seventeen, I'd lock myself away for hours at a time, days on end, with my Fender bass guitar. I still remember being awe-inspired by the great Abraham Laboriel. He did things on the bass I didn't know were possible. Keen to learn Laboriel's techniques, I discovered the power of listening and imitation as I played along with recordings, learning the bass line in small sections as I rewound and listened to him over and over again.

Professional jazz guitarist and educator Brent Vaartstra notes that, "Jazz is a language. One of the most important parts of learning a language is *mimicking*. You hear something and copy it. If you ask almost anybody who is bilingual, they will tell you they became fluent by immersing themselves with native speakers and being forced to listen, decipher and respond."[1] In fact, I distinctly remember being given sheet music when I was first in a jazz band in high school and how awkward and disingenuous it felt to play it "straight." Vaartstra goes on to state: "Jazz is not music that is meant to be learned from sheet music. It never was. Back in the bebop days in the 1940s, jazz musicians would pile into clubs and listen to each other play. They would literally pick things up on the bandstand, in rehearsals, and by just listening to records. ... *Jazz is first and foremost an aurally learned music.*"[2]

When it comes to jazz, there are musical standards and themes, and musicians spend a lifetime learning them. Once those patterns become second nature, the music comes alive as instrumentalists listen to one another, play together, and improvise.

What if effective leadership today is more like jazz? More like listening and improvising in the face of challenge and disruption?

I often think it would be nice if Jesus had written down some clear instructions for certain scenarios. We could open the "sheet music" Jesus provides, check the date, and simply play the notes precisely as he prescribed for a particular day and situation. There is no such sheet music, though, because we are not following rules or prescriptions. Instead, we are in a real relationship with Jesus and with one another, and we must learn to listen, discern, and improvise if we are to find our way through the challenges we face.

In Acts 6, the early church suddenly finds itself in a crisis. (Perhaps they too wished for some sheet music from Jesus.) A group of people, Hellenists, approach the Twelve and ask for help.[3] Up to this point, community members have been sharing everything in common.[4] While it seems all has been going well, the Hellenists explain that some of their women—their widows—are being overlooked in the distribution of food. Imagine how the apostles felt. They'd been entrusted with this early church; Christ had handed this off to them. And now there's a problem.

Jesus seems to have had total trust in the capacity of his followers to discern what the Spirit of God wanted them to do in the midst of a context and a situation that was radically different from anything any of them had previously encountered.[5]

So, imagine you are one of the Twelve, looking for a solution to this challenge. It appears to be a culturally-related issue—the Aramaic-speaking Jews are not being overlooked, yet the Hellenists, who were probably the Greek-speaking Jews, are. As is usually the case, the linguistic differences would likely also mean cultural differences, but all of you who are currently leading are Aramaic-speaking Jews. So what do you do?

Look at how the apostles respond. *They give the problem back to the people.*[6] By position, they may have been the *right* people to handle the situation, but by context and experience, they were the *wrong* people. And so they say, "Select from among yourselves" (Acts 6:3) for "It is not right that we should neglect the word of God in order to wait on tables" (Acts 6:2). Some have assumed the apostles' response is rooted in arrogance; that they saw themselves above the menial task of getting their hands dirty. But that's not how I read this passage. Their approach seems to arise from two key convictions. First, they were clear in their own specific calling and understood they must remain focused in order to be effective. Second, I believe they were discerning a way to expand the ministry and leadership capacities of this new community of faith. I imagine the apostles thinking, *If we handle this issue, we'll have to handle the next one. And the next one. And the next one after that. And that assumes that we are the best ones to decide what to do. But even if we are, what is the consequence of us hoarding the leadership at this stage?*

I have read this passage many times, but it took me a long time to catch on to the fact that they gave the problem back to the people. If you look at the text, you'll notice that the seven deacons (servant leaders) who are raised up to deal with the issue do not have Jewish names. They all have Greek names.[7] There are now more than just Aramaic-speaking Jewish leaders in this multi-cultural church. They now have multi-cultural leadership to face their challenges! And why?

Kenosis.

KENOSIS

Tales of descent and ascent are everywhere in the books, stories, and movies that capture our attention. From *Cinderella* to *Oliver Twist* to the farm boy Westley in *The Princess Bride,* key characters must take the journey of descent and humiliation but are ultimately exalted. One of my favorite examples of this is Neo in *The Matrix.*[8] Neo willingly descends into the matrix to rescue his friend, Morpheus, who is leading a rebellion. While Neo fights valiantly, he ultimately lays down his own life for his friend. As Bruce M. Fisk writes,

> But the story doesn't end there, for at this point Trinity, the woman in Neo's life, realizes her affection for him. She embraces his lifeless body,

and the sheer power of her love brings him back to life. Now, in his glori-
fied, resurrected state, Neo no longer finds himself vulnerable to the at-
tacks of the enemy. Now he is super-human, you might even say divine.
So The Matrix is another story of descensus and ascensus. The noble Neo
humbles himself, to the point of death, only to be liberated from death
and exalted once again. Another perilous journey downward is followed
by a glorious journey up again.[9]

This theme of descent and ascent is rooted in Scripture. Jesus embodied it in becoming human and then did so again as he "emptied himself" of privilege, leaving everything behind and taking on the nature of a servant for our sake. The Greek word for this emptying is kenosis. And it is this way of life that Paul invites the Christians in Philippi to imitate:

If you have any encouragement from being united with Christ, if any
comfort from his love, if any common sharing in the Spirit, if any ten-
derness and compassion, then make my joy complete by being like-
minded, having the same love, being one in spirit and of one mind. Do
nothing out of selfish ambition or vain conceit. Rather, in humility value
others above yourselves, not looking to your own interests but each of you
to the interests of the others.

Philippians 2:1–4 NIV

Let the same mind be in you that was in Christ Jesus,

> *who, though he was in the form of God,*
> *did not regard equality with God*
> *as something to be exploited,*
> *but emptied himself,*
> *taking the form of a slave,*
> *being born in human likeness.*
> *And being found in human form,*
> *he humbled himself*
> *and became obedient to the point of death—*

even death on a cross.
Therefore God also highly exalted him
and gave him the name
that is above every name,
so that at the name of Jesus
every knee should bend,
in heaven and on earth and under the earth,
and every tongue should confess
that Jesus Christ is Lord,
to the glory of God the Father.

Philippians 2:5–11

What would it have been like to hear this letter from the Apostle Paul … to read it for the very first time? Paul's churches were full of humans—just like ours. There was dysfunction, disunity, frustration, lack of alignment, lack of focus, and the church's leaders were facing challenges that no one knew how to handle.

And it's into this reality, that Paul writes, have you gotten anything at all out of following Christ? Has his love made any difference in your life? Does being in a community of the Spirit mean anything to you? Do you have a heart? Do you care?[10]

Paul is appealing to the Philippians. He wanted the very mind and way of Jesus to be embodied in the lives of everyday believers. He seemed to think that this was possible for every Christian, because the very same Spirit that raised Christ from the dead is in each of us. This is not just an aspiration or a vague hope. It is indeed how Paul envisioned the local church functioning; the way he envisioned disciples functioning—*together*.

And what does it mean to have the mind of Christ? What is it about Christ that Paul is particularly asking us to imitate or mimic here? At the heart of these verses, Paul is asking followers of Jesus to *empty themselves*. This is what it means to embody kenosis; and it flies in the face of our current solo-heroic paradigm of leadership, because when we truly embrace kenosis, we adopt the posture of a *servant*, not a *hero*. As leaders practice kenosis, we listen more than we talk. We operate in obedience to God and his will rather than pushing our own agenda. We become more concerned with "we" than "me." We look to the needs of others.

When we have this understanding of kenosis, we can see how those early Apostles in Acts 6 embodied its essence. Although the early church was experiencing great growth and becoming a Jesus movement, the Apostles were not trying to demonstrate their competence or impress others. It wasn't about them.[11] The central dynamic in any true Jesus movement is that Jesus is Lord,[12] and Jesus was their confession and core passion. As they faced challenges and made decisions, they were able to lead in humility and with confidence because they had experienced union with Christ Jesus, the love of God, and the fellowship of the Spirit. Their security was found in these realities.

UNION PRECEDES KENOSIS

There is a reason the beginning of Philippians 2 repeatedly uses the word "if"—"if … any encouragement," "if any comfort," "if any tenderness and compassion"—because the clauses are conditional. Kenosis can only come out of the context of being united with Christ. We can only operate with this level of self-emptying through God's power. Have you ever tried to lead and serve others in your own strength, outside of abiding in Christ[13] or out of step with the Spirit?[14] I know I have. It's an easy mistake to make. Musically, this would be like playing out of time with others or using untuned instruments. It sounds awful. Our kenosis—our service to others, our leadership with others—all must come out of the context of us being united with Christ. Paul is reminding his listeners of this so that our ministry—our leadership—doesn't turn out to be all about us.

Let's look at another scene in the book of Acts. There is arguing, passion, deliberation, prayer. Both Jews and non-Jews are in the room, and you are trying to make an extraordinarily difficult decision. Do you make the Gentiles follow Mosaic Law in order to remain Christians? The apostles and the elders debate heatedly. After everyone has finished talking, James, speaking on behalf of those gathered, announces the decision: to not put roadblocks in the way of the Gentiles who are turning to God. With everyone in agreement, they compose a letter to the Gentile believers, which includes these powerful words: "It seemed good to the Holy Spirit and to us ... " (Acts 15:28 NIV). Notice that it was the Holy Spirit who gave them discernment. Notice as well the "us." They were listening to the Spirit's music and *leading together.*

In the Old Testament we repeatedly read, "Thus saith the Lord." But in the New Testament it becomes, "It seemed good to the Holy Spirit and to us ...." I don't know about you, but most of the time I would prefer "Thus saith the Lord." I'd like the sheet music rather than learning to listen to jazz and play along. Sometimes we simply want an easy answer to a challenging circumstance; sometimes we are not confident in our ability to personally hear the voice of the Lord. Discernment, though, happens best when we are in tune with God, *together.* I wonder what would have happened if only Peter had made this decision. Or only Paul. Or only Barnabas. Or only any one of them. In this scene, they *discerned together* with the Holy Spirit what seemed good. And it was only possible because they were first united with Christ.

KENOSIS ASSUMES LETTING GO

When a doctor isn't sure what to do in a particular situation, they should never simply resort to saying what the patient wants to hear—or faking their way through. Consider how much better the outcome is when doctors are humble and honest enough to admit they don't know how to fix a problem; when they let go of their own image and control and invite people to work together to find solutions. Think of what it would look like for a medical doctor to gather a team of diverse medical professionals and sit down with a family and say, "We don't know what to do, but we are going to work on it with you—together."[15] In this scenario the mission has become more important than any person. Doing this requires courage, humility ... kenosis. And for somebody to practice kenosis in their leadership, they must be secure in who they are in Jesus.

The challenges the early church faced in Acts 6 and Acts 15 qualify for what modern-day sociologists describe as adaptive challenges,[16] and therefore required adaptive leadership. Ronald Heifetz from Harvard Business School delineates between what he calls *technical* leadership and *adaptive* leadership. Technical leadership relates to those challenges we already know how to deal with. In light of that, the task of implementing a solution is given to the respective experts.[17] For example, if my car breaks down, I simply take it to a mechanic, who already knows how to fix it. If I were to have to fix it myself, it would be an adaptive challenge because I would have to change and learn in order to come up with a solution. However, that is unnecessary because there are indeed experts who know what to do. Technical challenges require a technical kind of leadership.

Adaptive leadership, on the other hand, is required when we face challenges that we don't know what to do with. We have all lived through the COVID-19 pandemic—an adaptive challenge, as our context changed overnight, and we were faced with many unknowns. People, families, churches, hospitals, organizations, and even governments all had to adapt. There is no easy answer to these kinds of challenges. In fact, the title of Heifetz's first book on this subject is called *Leadership Without Easy Answers*.

When facing adaptive challenges, our instinct is to treat them like technical challenges. We act as if we have the expertise to make the decisions, and as a result we come up with *easy* solutions for *complex* situations. According to Heifetz, we can expect one of several outcomes when we try to use technical leadership within adaptive challenges. Sometimes organizations kick out the leader in the hope that a replacement will fix the problem (which, of course, almost never works). At other times, leaders cave to expectations—either their own or those around them—and fake their way through the challenge, pretending they know what they're doing.[18]

By contrast, look at how the early church leaders are operating in Acts 6 and Acts 15. Because they are facing an adaptive challenge that requires more than their current expertise, they embody kenosis by letting go of control and trusting both God and others around them to come up with a solution. As Heifetz would recommend, they gave the problem and the work back to the people.[19]

Though the biblical writers clearly didn't call it *adaptive leadership*, Acts 6, Philippians 2, and Acts 15 all illustrate what Heifetz has learned, and the practices commonly associated with adaptive leadership theory can actually be found all throughout Scripture.

There is never a one-size-fits-all solution to an adaptive challenge. The approach in one context might be radically different in another. Why?

Because our culture is different, our context is different, our people are different, our season is different, and we are reliant on the Spirit to help us discern what to do next. When we are facing adaptive challenges, we have to be willing to experiment our way into a new reality. We may make a mistake or two or three or ten or twenty—and we need the humility to apologize when things don't turn out the way we intended. In doing so, we demonstrate kenosis—we let go of our own agendas; we let go of control.

Letting go of control requires humility and trust in God. It also requires us to trust and empower others. This is what the early church leaders in Acts 6 and Acts 15 modeled for their community and for us. They intentionally invited others into the challenges with them rather than using the situation as an opportunity to demonstrate their own competence. They made decisions that were best for the mission and for the community at large—and what emerged was shared spiritual leadership.

BETTER TOGETHER

According to Rosamund and Benjamin Zander, leadership is "the art of possibility," and they use the metaphor of a symphony to describe it. The word *symphony* means "sounding together." In a symphony orchestra, the power is not in the individual voices or instruments but in all the diverse voices sounding together. The conductor in this metaphor—the only musician who is silent—depends on the ability to awaken possibility and empower those in the symphony whom he or she leads.[20]

Overcoming adaptive challenges requires shared leadership and "sounding together," because no single leader is smart enough to figure everything out alone. None of us have enough intellect, experience, capacity, or resources by ourselves. And it's impossible for one leader to be on top of all the complexities of any of the adaptive situations we've already explored. Yet, as a senior pastor or leader, we often hold the false belief that the responsibility to make decisions lies with us alone. Unfortunately, this expectation is frequently held by those in the congregation or organization as well.

If *I* make the decision, what happens the next time? I have to do it again. And again. And again. If the disciples in Acts 6 had made the decision about the Hellenists that day, a multicultural church would have continued to be led by a monocultural set of leaders. It would also have created a leadership bottleneck: Every time the people faced a problem, they would need to return to the Apostles for the solution.

Think about what actually happened, though. Deacons (servants) were raised up, and they were full of the Spirit and wisdom. Not only that, but the group included two individuals who became two of the most significant leaders in the early church: Stephen—who preached arguably the best sermon in history outside of the Sermon on the Mount, and as a result was our first martyr;[21] and Philip—who, in a stream of unlikely, supernatural events, took the gospel to Ethiopia.[22] None of this was in anybody's strategic plan. (Except perhaps in God's.) The Apostles were simply responding to the context and trying to discern what seemed good to the Holy Spirit and to them.

If the Apostles hadn't chosen shared leadership in Acts 6, would Acts 7 and following even have happened? We'll never know, but it certainly seems less likely. In those chapters, spiritual leadership expands beyond the Twelve. This didn't change the Apostle's *position* of leadership, but it did change their *role* of leadership.

Kenosis is demonstrated when, as individuals, we are in union with Christ and in step with the Spirit; and when we are walking in step with the Spirit *together* as a set of leaders. I get the image here of a great jazz ensemble—where there is competence, confidence, and humility; where the musicians listen well to one another and take turns improvising; where each instrumentalist both leads and follows as they are carried along by the music. When we operate like this in shared spiritual leadership, we no longer have anything to prove. Each of us can be confident we are made in the image of God, so we can let go of control. We see this in the life of Jesus, and at points in the life of Peter, Paul, and others in the early church.

However, letting go of control doesn't mean we let go of all responsibility. Recently, MyLinda and I faced a decision that would impact our entire family. We consulted with our children and prayed with them in the decision-making process. We asked them about how potential alternatives would make them feel. We invited their opinions and even made room for their grief and anger. Ultimately, as parents, we made the decision because our children did not yet have the maturity to do so. In the same way, adaptive leadership requires a discernment process, and we will explore this process in chapter eight.

FROM HERO TO KENOSIS

Many films and comics are all about the hero swooping in at the last moment to save the day. One of my personal favorites is Wonder Woman. An Amazonian princess, she is raised and trained on a sheltered island to become a warrior. As conflict rages in the outside world, she leaves her home to fight alongside normal humans in the war to end all wars. Just when it appears she will be defeated by the god of war, she prevails, and the result is peace on earth. In the process, she discovers her full powers and true destiny.[23]

Charismatic leadership theory espoused the importance of the solo-heroic leader and demonstrated that many such leaders emerge during challenging circumstances or crises. In such times, the leader rides in on a white horse and attempts to save the day. If they are successful, they become the hero.[24] On the other hand, when the solo-heroic leader rides in on a white horse and fails, s/he becomes the scapegoat, and the organization or culture learns nothing. They simply kick that leader out in hopes that the next one can save the day.

None of us are superheroes, but we do long for the world to change. If we have a *need* to be the hero, then we are not embodying kenosis, and it's essential we return to Philippians 2:1–3. (Have you been united with Christ? Is there any fellowship with the Spirit?) We must be united with Christ if we are to ensure that our leadership doesn't become about ourselves.

If we are indeed united with Christ, then we can be led to true kenosis. As we empty ourselves, our life and leadership can more truly reflect Christlike service, and we can indeed see world-transforming fruit. This only happens when we let go of control, truly trust God, and empower others. We'll have more to say about this notion of kenosis in chapter six as we look at the principle of becoming a spiritual leader.

CULTURAL ARCHITECTS

According to Barna research, the number of adults in the United States with a biblical worldview is only around 4 percent.[25] The US has become a mission field. And in most places, we are addressing this in the same way we always have—apparently, not very effectively. This is an adaptive challenge; and if, as a leader, I think I've got to figure it out myself, then we are all in trouble.

The role of leadership requires both humility and courage. It requires humility (kenosis) to name the challenge, admit that I can't solve it alone, and invite those full of the Spirit and wisdom into the discernment process.[26] And it requires courage to shift our leadership role from always being the one who makes decisions to creating the environment within which those decisions are made. A good leader is the *cultural architect*. Leaders don't change everything in these complex contexts, but they do create the culture (environment) in which transformation becomes possible. They initiate something that eventually changes everything. After modeling union and kenosis ourselves, I believe creating and shaping the culture is the most important role that leaders play.

We will return to this key principle of creating culture (environments) in chapter seven. For now, it is enough to say that overcoming adaptive challenges requires creating a culture of shared leadership.

Back to Philippians 2. Do you identify with Paul's admonition here? What would it look like for you to "have the same mind as Christ Jesus" when facing the challenges in your life and ministry?

This same mind is one of kenosis. As Jesus demonstrated, we are invited to empty ourselves and serve others. As we see in the book of Acts, this kenosis is only possible if we are first united with Christ, but that opens the opportunity to expand the leadership capacity of others around us.

If you feel as if you are facing your adaptive challenges alone—perhaps you're stuck in a solo-heroic leader paradigm—there is hope. Instead of looking for sheet music, take Jesus' invitation. Follow his lead and join in the symphony of shared leadership.

2

SOLOING AND SUPPORTING: THE MYTH OF THE SOLO-HEROIC LEADER

In the 2013 movie *Iron Man 3*, Iron Man (aka Tony Stark) finds himself needing the help of a young boy:

Boy: *"You're welcome."*

Tony Stark: *"For what? Did I miss something?"*

Boy: *"Me saving your life."*

Tony Stark: *"Yeah? A: saved you first. B: thanks—sort of. And C: if you do someone a solid don't be a yutz alright—just play it cool. Otherwise, you just come off grandiose."*

Boy: *"Unlike you? Admit it, we're connected."*

Tony Stark: *"What I need is for you to go home … You feel that? We're done here. Move out of the way or I'm gonna run you over. Bye kid … I'm sorry kid. You did good."*[1]

Iron man is the archetypal solo-heroic leader. No doubt you're familiar with the type: the superbly gifted, courageous, often reckless, arrogant, detached, lone genius. In countless scenes throughout the comics and movies, Iron Man needs help but prefers to solve the world's biggest problems by himself.

Others come to his aid, yet he refuses to acknowledge his need for help and insists on hoarding the glory for any successes. As a result, others often feel small around him.

We admire Iron Man's courage and are inspired by his genius, but most of us end up feeling sorry for this lonely, self-absorbed character.

A PASTOR'S JOURNEY

Jorge Acevedo, lead pastor of Grace Church in Fort Myers, Florida, is one of the most remarkable leaders I know, and Grace Church now has multiple growing campuses and a culture in which lives are continually being transformed. [2]

But this wasn't always the case. On the surface, Jorge might not have seemed like Iron Man, but he was acting as a gifted, courageous, lone genius. While Jorge acknowledges the move of God's Spirit in his first decade of leadership, much was dependent on the force of his gifts and personality. In those days, the church saw a dramatic increase in weekly worship attendance, many new converts to the faith, growth of the staff, expansion of budgets and programs, and a positive impact on the community. As a leader, Jorge even received awards as a distinguished evangelist with the fastest-growing church in his denomination. At the same time, though, he struggled in his personal life, and the church was "a mile wide and an inch deep." There was no agreed-upon system for growing disciples, the church experienced numerical growth instead of health, and the growth they did have was not sustainable. Jorge was burning out and beginning the slow, agonizing death of a solo-heroic leader.

Describing his life and leadership at the time, he said:

> When I hit bottom, we had been doing recovery ministry for six years. One of my family members was in recovery and went into rehab. Only then did I name my own addictions. I realized I had a performance addiction I'd been chasing my whole life, which led to me being a workaholic and a solo-heroic leader. Everything on the surface looked great, but in my inner world I was worn thin. Pastors

quit or fall because they don't see another way out. I felt the fire, and
I wanted out. [3]

SOLOING ... BUT NOT ALONE

Most of us enjoy hearing beautiful solos. Whether it's an amazing vocal, a stellar lead guitar, or a jaw-dropping saxophone in a jazz group, there is nothing quite like it. My friend David recently told me how much he loves listening to Yo-Yo Ma play J. S. Bach's unaccompanied cello suites. Ma possesses a command and sensitivity to the music that breathes new life into the century-old masterpieces. Bach's suites without Ma would still be masterpieces, and Ma without Bach would still be a virtuoso; but when they are combined any attempt to describe them fails to capture the beauty, pathos, passion, and energy that are communicated. However, for Ma and most other musicians, soloing is not the first choice. Most prefer the relational nature of performing with others.

That's why Yo-Yo Ma formed the Silk Road ensemble with musicians from various cultures around the world. When they create music together, Ma describes the process in terms of "generous virtuosity." Musicians, gifted in their own cultures, open-handedly share the musical ideas they have mastered with other musicians who will reinterpret them through the lens of their musical traditions and training. Ultimately, all music and musicians inherently seek to exemplify the value Yo-Yo Ma describes as "generous virtuosity." Music isn't simply something to be mastered, but something to be shared—among the musicians creating the music, in intimate gatherings and on grand stages, from generation to generation and across the ages.[4]

I am fascinated by Frank Barrett's comparison of effective leadership and jazz performance. In most jazz numbers, solos rotate from instrument to instrument, which allows each musician to both lead and follow, to both solo and support.[5] This is quite different from the paradigm of solo-heroic leadership, where the attention is often given to leaders as individual heroes.

Many of us have lived under the myth that the solo-heroic manner is the most effective way to lead. Is it though? Maybe we would be better served and better serve others by sharing leadership in both soloing and supporting.

CHARACTERISTICS OF THE SOLO-HEROIC LEADER

When I was a freshman in college, I vividly remember a concert in which an extremely talented upper classman burst into a solo during a number that didn't call for one. It was a humbling lesson—for all of us.

Many of us have seen solo-heroic leadership modeled, even though we may not have classed it as such. In fact, we may have a difficult time imagining any other way to lead. Perhaps this is due in part to our desire to get things done quickly. We know intuitively that it is often more efficient to just do something ourselves rather than take time to involve others. It can be challenging to even imagine leading in any other way.

We may even personally exhibit some of the characteristics of solo-heroic leadership ourselves, but we discount them because we don't see them rising to the level of the solo-heroic caricature. We don't tend to think of ourselves, for example, as the consciously evil, power-hungry villain. However, I encourage you to identify how these tendencies appear in your own leadership, even in subtle, inadvertent ways.

Here are three key characteristics and patterns of solo-heroic leaders:

- A desire for control
- A reliance on giftedness, experience, and intuition
- A tendency toward narcissism

A DESIRE FOR CONTROL

I once knew of a church planter who emphasized the importance of teams in his new church but consistently invited inexperienced people into leadership. While I believe this was primarily a series of subconscious choices, the net result was that he created an environment where all decision-making relied on his expertise. He gave others trivial tasks to complete—such as setting up for the service each week—but he hesitated to delegate any true responsibility or authority. His own desire for control worked against his articulated value of team, and eventually many of the strongest leaders in his church left.

The solo-heroic leader's desire for control is often based in fear. A leader who is afraid of looking less competent than others may intentionally or subconsciously make all the important decisions. We may even convince ourselves that making all of the decisions is our responsibility, justifying our solo-heroic patterns with biblical examples.

The solo-heroic leader often equates authority with *position*, and influence with *title*. This causes us to fall prey to the misperception that sharing authority limits our influence; and this naturally leads to a desire to control so as not to lose authority.

Further, this desire for control is often accompanied by a desire for *power*. Often this power is connected to the position we hold, which might be linked to an official title or a role we play. For instance, every parent has power by nature of our role, but we have a choice in whether we use our power to control or to empower our children. Remember Jesus' words: "You know that the rulers of the Gentiles lord it over them, and their great ones are tyrants over them" (Matthew 20:25b). When we "lord over others," we abuse our power. One of my mentors once told me he felt convicted to never again respond to an inquiry from his children with the phrase, "Because I said so." In his mind, this response was simply a way of "lording it over" his own children—asserting the power of his role over and above anything else.

When we choose to assert control, we often resort to manipulation. By his own admission, a pastor friend of mine consistently displays anger or frustration in staff meetings in order to get people to back down and give in to him. He also has a tendency to micromanage the strategies of his staff in order to get them to do things the way he prefers rather than in ways they might choose.

A hierarchical approach to leadership can add fuel to the fire, exacerbating the control tendencies of the solo-heroic leader. In their book *The Church as Movement,* J. R. Woodward and Dan White, Jr., suggest that "a hierarchical approach to leadership lends itself to controlling leadership …. It often leads to a more passive, needy, consumeristic people and often a less Christlike leader in the end."[6]

When there is a hierarchy already in place, the solo-heroic leader utilizes that structure as a means of controlling both people and outcomes. When there is not already such a structure in place, or if the structure does not lend itself to strong control, solo-heroic leaders will often work to establish a rigid hierarchy. In one church I was coaching, the church leaders had worked for many months to develop a culture of shared vision and values, along with a system to develop and multiply disciples and leaders. In the midst of these transitions, a new pastor came. Though he said all the right things to convince the church he was in favor of shared leadership, he subsequently worked to undo everything the team and church had built. It wasn't long before the church was even more hierarchical than it had been before.

In our leadership, most of us have control tendencies that we do not care to admit or perhaps do not even see.

Self-check: Do I tend to control or empower? Why is this the case?

A RELIANCE ON GIFTEDNESS, EXPERIENCE, AND INTUITION

Solo-heroic leaders often rely primarily on our own giftedness, experience, and intuition. Clearly our giftedness comes from the Lord, and we do well to function within it; but we typically over-rely on these attributes to the detriment of our people and organization. For example, if we function as if we are the only ones with vision, we position ourselves as the sole vision caster and others around us as merely the implementors of that vision. Woodward and White state:

> The senior pastor receives a vision and then works to get people on board with it .... It looks strangely similar to the CEO business model. What kind of people does this produce? Or what do businesses seek to create? Consumers![7]

If we are extraordinarily gifted as solo-heroic leaders, we may be able to persuade others easily. In fact, we may assume that this ability to persuade is our primary role as a leader, and we may utilize it in our vision-casting, preaching, decision-making, and recruiting. While we may use that persuasive ability to recruit others to the cause, this seldom leads to leaning into the adaptive challenges facing the organization because solo-heroic leaders do not wish to appear incompetent by naming challenges or asking for help. This dynamic creates a co-dependency on the leader. Over time, many in the organization may view the solo-heroic leader as a micromanager—and often as one who lacks follow-through, because it is impossible for the leader to accomplish the stated vision alone. When this pattern continues, it creates a lack of trust.

Even when the intuition of the solo-heroic leader is right—arising from giftedness and experience—s/he may be unable to explain where the intuition came from or how s/he knew what to do in a given situation. In coaching highly intuitive leaders, I have often asked, "Could you equip someone to do what you just did?" Unfortunately, the answer is almost always no. Without the ability to equip others to do what we do, nothing can scale beyond the solo-heroic leader.

When we practice this type of leadership, we tend to assume that *my* idea is always the best one in the room. Admitting that someone else has a better idea is difficult, if not impossible; and allowing someone else's idea to be implemented threatens our ego. More often than not, we will pursue our own ideas over the ideas of others.

Self-check: As I think about my own story, where have I fallen into this trap of relying too heavily on my own giftedness, experience, and intuition?

A TENDENCY TOWARD NARCISSISM

One evangelist friend of mine loved to preach and see people flood the altar in response to his messages. His goal was to see souls saved, but seldom did he invest time in building relationships with his listeners. Eventually he felt convicted by the Lord to love those *to whom* he preached as much as he loved *preaching itself*. To his credit—and by means of God's grace—he began to do that, and he and his leadership was transformed. But his initial tendency was typical of a solo-heroic leader. When we drift into this type of leadership, we put ourselves at the center of our own universe. Other people are all too often seen as the means to an end that we, as the leader, have in mind. And relationships are sacrificed on the altar of success.

Throughout this chapter I have referenced the notion of heroism as entirely negative. The world certainly needs heroes who sacrifice for the sake of others and for the sake of mission. Jesus is this type of hero, as we saw in Philippians 2. That being said, solo-heroic leaders do not generally follow this pattern. Instead, they are motivated by two self-referential extremes: *ego* and *insecurity*. All of us can veer toward one extreme or another.

The *ego* extreme does not require detailed description, and it is easy to identify how it is narcissistic. There are church leaders, for instance, who will not even allow others in their office and act as a king among peasants. They refuse to listen to others and claim they are accountable to God alone. They enjoy attention and may secretly—or openly—expect the world to revolve around them (picture Iron Man). Most of us have interacted with this type of leader, and it has left a sour taste in our mouths.

Unfortunately, these traits are exalted in contemporary celebrity culture—with devastating effects. Dr. Jene Twenge's extensive research indicates today's young people may be more confident, open-minded, and ambitious, but they are also disengaged, narcissistic, distrustful, and anxious.[8] Many have lived with the illusion that they can be anything they want to be, and even our schools have often reinforced this message—giving everyone a trophy or a blue ribbon simply for participation rather than merit. The good intentions behind these strategies have led to a sense of entitlement … and, ironically, also to greater stress and depression. The consequences of acting as if the world revolves around young people don't surface until adulthood, when they face the cruel reality of the workforce, where their boss doesn't hold to the same view.

While the extreme caricature of the egomaniac may repulse us, ego often reveals itself in more subtle ways. As with my friend Jorge, we could have a performance addiction; or a desire for praise; or a drive to make a name for ourselves. But how can Jesus be Lord if we are at the center?

Narcissism can also manifest as *insecurity*. The narcissism of the insecure leader is not caused by their desire for attention—in fact, just the opposite. Paradoxically, the greater the leader's insecurity, the more likely they are to be self-focused, which is simply another form of narcissism.

That was my experience. As a young leader, even though I longed to reflect Jesus in every way, my insecurities unconsciously affected the way I lived and led. I was constantly worried about how others perceived me. I assumed others could easily see through my incompetence, so I wore a mask to cover up my true self. The mask often took the form of pretending everything was okay, when I was secretly struggling or constantly worrying about whether anyone actually liked me. Wearing this kind of mask led to greater and greater insecurity.

I also had unrealistic expectations of myself. If and when I failed, or did not perform up to my own internal standards, I could easily spiral into shame. And shame leads to hiding. Like Adam and Eve, I was afraid of being "found out" by God and by those I was leading. Notice how my insecurities were causing me to focus on myself more and more. This is just another form of narcissism.

When we are insecure, we end up leading in solo-heroic ways that are similar to our egotistical counterparts. This is especially true for those of us who have a desire to please people and have difficulty drawing boundaries or saying no. If left unchecked, this type of insecurity can lead to hoarding responsibility in an attempt to impress others or prove ourselves. Attention and praise can become a drug that the insecure, solo-heroic leader craves, and any failure can lead to depression. Like hiding, this depression is another by-product of shame—as insecure leaders are often unable to see themselves as God sees them. Insecure leaders—compelled by the opinions of others—may also succumb to compromising their own integrity in an attempt to please others.

Each of these solo-heroic leadership characteristics can lead to dysfunction in the teams and organizations we lead.

Self-check: Where do I see myself in these solo-heroic characteristics? What might the Lord want to transform in me?

CONSEQUENCES OF SOLO-HEROIC LEADERSHIP

In the first Avengers movie, Nick Fury assembles a team of superheroes to respond to a threat to Earth. Their combined superpowers offer great potential for shared leadership—but Iron Man actually works against it. In his arrogance and self-importance, Iron Man isolates himself and attempts to come up with his own solutions for the dangers facing humanity—almost as if the whole mission is a competition to win. His need for control limits not only his ability to trust others but also the possibilities that could be generated by other perspectives and joint energy given to the task.

What are the consequences of solo-heroic leadership that should concern us? Woodward and White state: "If everything meaningful about a church seems to disappear with one key person, leadership should be different."[9] As solo-heroic leaders, we may or may not be aware of the negative effect our leadership has on others.

Here are some of the most common consequences of solo-heroic leadership:

- Isolation
- Lack of repeatability
- Co-dependency
- Lack of trust
- Treating adaptive challenges as technical problems
- Choosing our own way

ISOLATION

One of my best friends and his wife served as missionaries in some of the most unreached places and challenging circumstances in the world. They are two of the most courageous people I have ever known, and my admiration for them cannot be overstated. While in a dark place, my friend found himself lured into sexual temptation, and he attempted to battle it alone. That temptation finally got the best of him in a solitary act that forced his family's relocation and consequently shaped the rest of his life.

He later shared this haunting reflection with me: "If I had told only one person I was struggling, everything might have been different." Ashamed of his struggle, he kept it to himself, assuming he was strong enough to fight temptation on his own. *He was not.*

Isolation is a dangerous place.

One of the things I hear most often from pastors and C-level leaders in organizations (i.e., CEO, CFO, COO, etc.) is how isolating leadership can be. Isolation breeds loneliness, depression—even scenarios such as my missionary friend found himself in.

It is often assumed that isolation just comes with the territory of leadership—the more senior we become as a leader, the lonelier we become. While this may be common, it is not healthy. Isolation is often a natural consequence of desiring control, relying on our own gifts, experience, and intuition, and living in a way that is self-focused. It can also be caused by uncertainty about whether or not we can trust others. We may even choose to distance ourselves from relationships because we are embarrassed to admit or allow others to see our own weaknesses.

Self-check: Am I lonely? Have I isolated myself from others? If so, why?

LACK OF REPEATABILITY

Addressing pastors and church leaders, Jim Collins, author of *Good to Great*, once said, "If you leave your church, and it declines in your absence, you have failed as a leader."[10]

This, unfortunately, is the story of far too many churches. Have you ever witnessed a church grow like crazy under a highly charismatic leader? Perhaps you've even been that leader. What happens when that leader leaves? Too often the cycles of growth and decline in a church can be mapped directly to the tenure of its pastor. When there is a strong, captivating leader at the helm, the church grows; and when there is not, the church declines. This clearly illustrates the impact that leadership—especially solo-heroic leadership—can have on the life of a church or other organization.

When there *is* success, the solo-heroic leader rarely takes the time and effort to actively reflect on patterns that have led to such success. As a result, s/he fails to equip the next generation of leaders to see similar breakthroughs. In Ephesians 4, the Apostle Paul paints a beautiful picture of the role of leaders in equipping others for the work of ministry. Equipping requires intentionality, yet the solo-heroic leader often misses the importance of this role.

Unfortunately, this lack of repeatability creates what can be described as a "negative reinforcing loop." In other words, the paradigm itself perpetuates even more solo-heroic leadership. When this is all that people see modeled, they assume it is the best, and perhaps only, way to lead.

Self-check: What would happen to my church or organization if something happened to me? Could things that are going well be repeated or even multiplied?

CO-DEPENDENCY

Remember my friend Jorge? In the first decade of his ministry at Grace Church, he inadvertently created a bottleneck by having a countless number of direct reports and by not empowering others to make decisions. Everyone and everything was dependent on him. The lack of repeatability associated with solo-heroic leadership within a staff or organization automatically results in co-dependency.

Co-dependency is an unhealthy behavioral condition in a relationship, and in the case of solo-heroic leadership, it means that no one in the organization is able to act unless they are given permission. (You're probably familiar with the classic examples: when an organization can't buy toilet paper without consulting the CEO or when a church can't pick out the color of carpet without the pastor in the room.)

Rather than operating in a more interdependent manner, when we function as solo-heroic leaders, we create systems—often intentionally—that are dependent upon us in order to function. In Jorge's case, he didn't want it to be this way, but it had become an unspoken value in the church as it grew.

We may find ourselves in an organization with a co-dependent culture that we did not create. If we inherit such a system from previous solo-heroic leaders, it can be extremely challenging to transition. In the absence of competence to change such a culture, many leaders fit into the norms within that system and eventually become solo-heroic by default.

Self-check: In my organization, is too much dependent upon me? Have we created systems that empower or disempower others?

LACK OF TRUST

Patrick Lencioni insists that trust is foundational to healthy organizations[11] and describes how a lack of trust can lead to unhealthy conflict, low commitment, a lack of accountability, and an inability to accomplish desired results.[12] Lencioni goes on to claim that invulnerability in leaders is linked to lack of trust. In other words, if we always act as if we have everything together and never demonstrate our own weakness or need for others, our people will likely distrust us over time. And they will not feel trusted by us.

When any of the solo-heroic characteristics we've discussed so far are in operation, there is invariably a lack of trust. Even if those in the organization have faith in the leader (after all, we can be perceived as a "hero"), the leader seldom releases any meaningful responsibility. We may trust the character of others around us, but we are unwilling to *entrust* them with much leadership or authority. This lack of trust in others may reveal, ultimately, a lack of trust in God.

When we lead in this way, we begin to assume that the success of our church or organization is entirely dependent upon us. The long-term results of such leadership can be dysfunction, if not devastation.

Think about this for a moment. We certainly want to see fruitfulness, and, as leaders, we likely have some clear outcomes in mind for our organizations. If Lencioni is right about trust being foundation to our healthy, our commitment, and fruitfulness, shouldn't we be more attuned to the trust barometer in our churches and organizations?

I've had countless conversations with pastors who continue to lead in solo-heroic ways and ignore this element of trust. One such pastor assumed there was high trust for him because no one ever challenged his leadership. It hadn't occurred to him that there was no context in which people could do so. He received positive feedback about his preaching and didn't think any deeper about how people perceived him. He saw himself as the one responsible for the ministry and thought of his lay people as spiritually immature and in need of him. What he didn't realize is that he was perceived as arrogant, untrusting, and as a control freak. His key leaders didn't trust him. When this finally blew up, his tenure at the church ended—and the congregation had a mess to clean up, including diminished witness in the community.

Self-check: How much do I entrust to others? Do we have an environment that is healthy enough to make it through conflict?

TREATING ADAPTIVE CHALLENGES AS TECHNICAL PROBLEMS

During the beginning stages of the COVID-19 pandemic, many church leaders spent considerable energy transitioning their ministries to online platforms. While I commend churches for attempting to innovate, many of these changes were technical and did not address the deep nature of the adaptive challenges at hand. Seldom were these leaders asking how such technical changes actually benefitted the church in achieving its stated mission or vision. Many leaders I interviewed and coached during this time expressed their exhaustion and the feeling that they were working more hours than ever before. When I pressed them on this, many admitted that they were managing the changes alone—rather than involving others. Some of this came from genuine pastoral concern not to burden others. Some of it arose from a desire to prove their leadership acumen during crisis. Some came from fear—of the unknown, of failure, or of looking incompetent. Whatever the reason, the result was to diminish the potential of true adaptive solutions that could come through shared leadership. Instead the focus went to simpler, albeit time-consuming, technical solutions to these complex challenges. Several of these pastoral leaders are actually proponents of shared leadership, but in the midst of the complexities of this particular adaptive challenge, they reverted to a solo-heroic paradigm.

Treating adaptive challenges as technical problems often keeps our churches and organizations stuck in their current reality with no hope of anything new. It also requires us to *fake* our way through these complex dynamics of leadership rather than openly admitting we don't have all the answers and inviting others into leadership with us.

Self-check: As I face adaptive challenges, what is my natural tendency? Do I just stay busy? Do I attempt to face it alone? Do I invite others into it with me? Why?

CHOOSING OUR OWN WAY

We're all aware of the many scandals that have surfaced among church leaders in recent years. From misuse of finances, to systematic abuse, to sexual misconduct, these scandals have divided churches and tarnished our witness. Though hopefully most of us will not abuse our power in such egregious ways, perhaps the most alarming consequence of solo-heroic leadership is that it tends to happen apart from grace; apart from the body of Christ.

Put another way, what influence does the Holy Spirit have on leadership and decision-making in the local church if everything is done by one leader? It could be that the leader is seeking God earnestly and attempting to be faithful but is not benefitting from the perspective offered by the community. Most scandals and leadership failures occur because leaders are not accountable to the community of faith. This is dangerous. When the Holy Spirit is not leading and there is no accountability, solo-heroic leaders can all too often build their own kingdoms rather than participating in Jesus' kingdom.

Self-check: Is Jesus truly Lord? Am I in step with the Spirit or simply following my own plans?

As we have discussed, leaders may be cognitively aware of these characteristics of solo-heroic leadership, or they may be blind spots. Regardless, when we function in these ways, we are unable to see the negative effects our actions are having on our ministries and organizations. Those around us, however, are often painfully aware—but may feel paralyzed and unsure of how to change or address them.

HOPE FOR TOMORROW

Though we may identify many of these solo-heroic traits in our own life and leadership, the good news is that tomorrow can be different. My own leadership journey is evidence of this.

Some years ago, a few dear friends were willing to risk their friendship with me in order to help me grow. Within a short period of time, multiple people confronted me about my pride—how much I focused on myself and how little I focused on others. I saw myself as loving and humble; as looking out for the interests of others. But those closest to me were saying just the opposite—it felt like a kick in the gut.

My first response was defensiveness. In fact, had I not been confronted multiple times, I might have just ignored those comments and justified myself. But clearly there was a pattern, and I had a choice to make. Was this really the person I wanted to be? I cried out for the Lord to change me. In answer to this cry, I was invited to join a discipleship group where I would eventually memorize Philippians 2:1–11 and would be accountable to grow in humility.

As I confessed earlier, my pride was caused by my insecurities. I used to think that we grow out of our insecurities over time, but I have learned, through my own experiences and through coaching many leaders, that we actually grow more *into* our insecurities. Rather than maturing, we allow our insecurities to increase until they become, in effect, our identity. As leaders, we can teach and preach a message that taunts us when we look in the mirror. All of this, if left unchecked, leads to greater insecurity. We can inadvertently end up extremely self-centered and self-focused. Whether it is based in our ego or our insecurities, self-orientation leads us to become solo-heroic leaders. This had become my story.

In his beautiful grace, though, the Lord allowed me to see just how my insecurities were affecting my relationships. In those moments, I began a journey of discovering humility, and it has completely changed my approach to God, to myself, to life, to others, and to leadership.

Early in this chapter I described my friend Jorge. He loves to tell the story of his three conversions. The first occurred when he was overcome by the grace and love of God and experienced a radical conversion to Jesus. His second conversion occurred after he'd been a pastor a while, when he fell in love with the church as God's instrument to bring hope to the world. His third conversion was from solo-heroic leader to generative team leader.[13]

I told you how Jorge's church was bottlenecked and co-dependent, and how he was struggling in his personal life. He was worn thin and looking for an escape. In desperation, Jorge invited his good friend and protégé, Wes Olds, to join the staff of Grace Church. As soon as he did, Jorge promptly left on vacation, putting Wes in charge. Wes had already been through his own transition from solo to team leadership and was immediately overwhelmed by how much activity and decision-making revolved around Jorge.

Upon Jorge's return, Wes recommended coaching, and Jorge's leadership transformation began. Jorge gained new capacities in disciple-making, spiritual leadership development, and ministry multiplication. *The transformation was profound.* Now, all ministry at Grace Church happens in teams; there is intentional focus and strategy around disciple-making; and there is health not merely growth. The investment in the vision of Grace Church is deeper and wider among their people, and they have greatly expanded their ministry. Jorge now has only four direct reports, and his ministry is multiplied in them as theirs is now multiplied in the leaders they work with. Moreover, Jorge explains, "My life is healthier and holier."

And what of my missionary friend—the one I mentioned earlier in the chapter? The tragic failure that could have been the end of everything of value in his life, instead turned out to be the beginning of something transformative. The guy who was once ashamed to admit he was struggling has now become one of the most vulnerable, grace-filled, humble, grateful followers of Jesus I know. This is the way the grace of God works in our lives.

If you recognize some of the solo-heroic leadership traits in your own life and leadership, it's not too late to change. God is always at work transforming his people.

The whole paradigm of solo-heroic leadership assumes that the leader is the smartest and most qualified person to lead in each situation, but the truth is that *we* is always smarter than *me*. In the coming chapter, we will explore the genius of shared leadership as seen in the Scriptures.

3

THE BEAUTY OF HARMONY: THAT THEY MAY BE ONE

"You're going to wear yourself out—and the people, too," Jethro told Moses. "This job is too heavy a burden for you to handle all by yourself."[1]

Ever found yourself in a similar position? Burdened by a job or a role that was too busy or too big to handle alone?

At this point in his life, Moses was acting as a judge. Exodus 18 tells us people came to him from morning to night, day after day, and he handled all of their disputes. Jethro—his father-in-law—encouraged Moses to pray for the people and equip them in God's ways. He also suggested that Moses share leadership. Not only would this help Moses lead more effectively, it would also be more sustainable. Following Jethro's advice, Moses chose "capable men" (Exodus 18:25 NIV) to handle part of his load.

This episode from the life of Moses gives us a glimpse not only of the importance of being humble enough to listen, but also the benefits that shared leadership can bring in overcoming burnout and multiplying impact.

In the previous chapter, I described my friend Jorge's journey—from a performance-addicted solo-heroic leader to a generative team leader. You may recall that in the midst of his perceived success, he was worn thin and looking for a way out. The Lord provided a way *through* instead. His friend Wes became his "Jethro"—facilitating his move toward shared leadership.

SHARED LEADERSHIP
THROUGHOUT SCRIPTURE

Let's look at some other examples of shared leadership in Scripture.

The joint stories of Ezra and Nehemiah provide a beautiful picture of partnership. These separate books of the Bible were originally a single work, written sometime in the early period of Greek occupation of Israel's land. Ezra was a priest, scribe, and scholar of the commandments of the Lord;[2] Nehemiah was a Persian official who worshipped God.[3] Ezra's concern was for the people of God to follow God's commandments, while Nehemiah worked to rebuild the walls of Jerusalem. Under the Spirit's inspiration and empowerment, Ezra the clergyman and Nehemiah the lay person worked together to restore God's people to his love and purposes—and the same is possible for us today.

Early on, in Jesus' ministry, he simply involved the disciples alongside him, as he modeled what to do. As time went on, and his disciples grew in maturity and relationship with him, Jesus increasingly invited them to lead alongside him. When Jesus instructed his disciples to feed the crowds,[4] he was giving them opportunity to step toward leadership, even though they were not yet ready. Jesus also sends out the Twelve with his own authority, and they began to act in the same ways they had seen Jesus act.[5] Ultimately, after his resurrection, Jesus commissions the disciples into the very same ministry he has embodied, making disciples.[6]

Acts 2 and 4 tell us that the early followers of Jesus clearly shared life together. They received the gift of the Holy Spirit, devoted themselves to God and to one another, followed the teaching of the apostles, and gave themselves to the breaking of bread and to prayer. They also consistently leaned on one another for discernment and leadership (as we saw in Acts 6 and 15). As the Spirit led them, they moved boldly into God's calling.

Throughout his entire mission and ministry, the Apostle Paul led alongside others, including Barnabas, Silas, Timothy, Mark, and Luke. And everywhere Paul planted a new community of Jesus' followers, he equipped and raised up a team of elders. In his calling as an Apostle, Paul seemed to always have his eye on the next frontier of mission, yet he chose to prioritize preparing leaders in each place before moving on. When those communities struggled, he not only wrote letters to encourage them but also sent along his own team to help them.

In Ephesians 4, Paul paints the picture of the unity of God and of the body of Christ and then reminds us that Christ gifted the church with apostles, prophets, evangelists, shepherds, and teachers (APEST) to equip the church. In order to grow into the fullness of Christ—displaying both unity and maturity—shared leadership is necessary; and all the different roles and functions of APEST should be represented. Paul seems to be indicating that Christ-gifted, Spirit-empowered shared leadership that is equipping the entire body of Christ is crucial to us fulfilling God's calling on the church.[7]

UNITY IS GOD'S DESIGN

Years ago, I was part of leading a worship service with more than six hundred college students present. We were doing a live recording that night, and my band had prepared well. At this point, we had been playing together multiple times a week for almost four years. Several of us had written the music, we had practiced like crazy, and we had already led most of these songs dozens of times prior to that evening.

During a song entitled "God is Great" (written by my brother Britt), all the energy and effort we had invested, along with the depth of relationship we had built as a team, somehow got infused with a fresh wind of the Holy Spirit. I felt as if we were transported to another place, as we rotated between soloing and supporting in beautiful harmony. In that moment, we all seemed to play and sing better than we were naturally capable of. To this day, as I listen to that recording, I relive that feeling and remember getting lost playing the bass guitar in passionate worship of Jesus with my friends. It was a palpable experience of unity.

Unity, as it turns out, is a critical component of effective shared spiritual leadership. It is not merely a tactical strategy for getting things done; it is rooted in the very nature and character of God. The Father, Son, and Holy Spirit are a community of unity, and this triune relationship embodies perfect love, hospitality, creativity, and shared purpose—all of which leads to generative, life-giving movement.[8]

And when we, as the body of Christ, exhibit this kind of unity, it is actually an expression of being made in the image of God.

Contrast this with the division so prevalent in society and even within organizations. It has become normal for people to work at cross purposes rather than toward a common goal. In fact, we see more than disunity; we have often become severely polarized.

Prior to his betrayal and arrest on his way to the cross, Jesus' final act was to pray for his disciples. He prayed not only for those following him on that day, but also for all who would ever follow him.[9]

And what did he pray?

Four times in his brief prayer, Jesus expresses his desire for us to be *one*.[10] And the oneness he is praying for is this: "That they may be one, as we are one" (John 17:22)—that *we* would be one in the same way the Father and Son are one.

What characterizes the oneness within the Trinity? In a word: *love*.

There is a reason love, particularly *agape* love, is described by Jesus and the New Testament writers as the sum of all the law and prophets.[11] It's because "God is love."[12] Love is not merely a characteristic that describes God but is God's very nature. Acting with the unity that exists within the Trinity means reflecting the very love of God. So Jesus specifically prays that his disciples (including us) would know that the Father loves us just as he loves Jesus and that this love would dwell in us.[13]

Remember, in Philippians 2, Paul's appeal for us to be united with Christ and to know the comfort of God's love? Paul is asking us to "be of the same mind, having the same love, being in full accord and of one mind" (Philippians 2:2). This is a plea for the same unity that Jesus prays for in John 17—the kind of unity that is rooted in love, particularly God's love, and results in being one in spirit and purpose.

Elsewhere, Paul writes,

I therefore, the prisoner in the Lord, beg you to lead a life worthy of the calling to which you have been called, with all humility and gentleness, with patience, bearing with one another in love, making every effort to maintain the unity of the Spirit in the bond of peace. There is one body and one Spirit, just as you were called to the one hope of your calling, one

Lord, one faith, one baptism, one God and Father of all, who is above all and through all and in all.

♪ Ephesians 4:1–6

Paul challenges—or perhaps more accurately *begs*—his listeners to live a life worthy of their calling in love and to make every effort to maintain the unity of the Spirit. He then goes on to remind us of the oneness in God and in the body of Christ.

All of this points to unity as God's design, both for relationships and for shared leadership. It is not merely having consensus around what to do; it is living in unity with God and with one another, deeply rooted in the love of God and embodying a shared purpose. This life with God and one another is precisely what we see in each of the biblical examples described earlier.

The purposes of this unity must be *God's purposes*, otherwise the results can be destructive. Genesis 11 tells us the interesting story of the Tower of Babel. We learn that the whole earth had one language, and the people united together to build a tower to the heavens. It seems one of their primary motivations was to "make a name for [them]selves" (Genesis 11:4). Notice God's response:

And the LORD said, "Look, they are one people, and they have all one language; and this is only the beginning of what they will do; nothing that they propose to do will now be impossible for them. Come, let us go down, and confuse their language there, so that they will not understand one another's speech." So the LORD scattered them abroad from there over the face of all the earth, and they left off building the city.

Genesis 11:6–8

The people are unified in purpose, but it is not God's purpose. Their motive is to exalt themselves, and God says that "nothing that they propose to do will now be impossible for them" (v. 6). God is so concerned about their alignment with one another rather than him, that he separates them.

Human leaders (sometimes prompted by their own evil desires and sometimes influenced by the enemy) can utilize the power of unity for their own purposes. Adolf Hitler is a clear example of this. We see much destruction in our world from this kind of "make a name for ourselves" type of leadership. This is why it is so critical to embody the kind of unity that we see in the Trinity—unity that links relationship in love *and* shared purpose.

THE BIBLICAL MODEL OF THE BOTH/AND

Dr. Michelle Buck, clinical professor of leadership at Northwestern University, explains that it is "human nature to think in terms of 'either/or'... The ability to embrace complexity and even paradox may be a key ingredient for both reducing polarization and generating greater unity in society and for managing stress and well-being during a crisis."[14]

In organizational contexts, either/or thinking always limits options, while both/and thinking expands possibilities. In their book *Reframation*, Alan Hirsch and Mark Nelson discuss our tendency toward reductionist thinking:

> *The alternative to reductionist thinking ... is to ... cultivate an ability to embrace multiple possibilities at the same time. Instead of choosing between A or B, we are to figure out a way to have both A and B. In other words, we resolve our problems not by more analysis but by synthesis. We need to always think bigger ... never smaller. ... It is this symphonic way of thinking ... that connects the dots, opens doors, and cleanses perceptions to enable us to really see again.*[15]

Many of us live in cultural contexts with a worldview that makes it difficult to hold paradoxes in tension. We tend to think only in either/or categories, whether that be about theology, politics, education, or even leadership. From a biblical perspective though, humans were made both for *relationship* (love) with God and one another *and* for *responsibility* (purpose). From Creation, God made humanity in his own image to enjoy relationship and be fruitful, as well as to subdue and have dominion upon the earth.[16]

Yet, consider the activities of the average church. We tend to either have missional purpose aimed at those outside the church *or* relational connection with God and others within the church. We are either focused on outward-facing activities, trying to reach those who don't yet know Jesus; *or* we are engaged in worship and small-group activities, which tend to focus on forming and building relationship with other believers. Clearly both/and is healthier than either/or in this example.

Or think for a moment about the distinction between committees and small groups in the local church. In a committee (at least in a healthy version of committees or church boards), diverse perspectives are heard, decisions are made, and mission-focused action happens as a result. In small groups, relationships grow, and people are spiritually formed. If either of these occur without the other, however, it is impossible to fulfill the both/and mission of the local church.

What if Jesus had set up his ministry in this either/or way? What if he chose twelve individuals to fulfill the missional purpose with him and twelve others as a small group to be his friends and grow in grace together? The idea is absurd. First, everything would take twice as long. Second, the disciples he was closest to would have no involvement in the work Jesus was about. Third, those working closest with Jesus in mission would have little context for trust, given a lack of relational and formational focus, which would dramatically affect their ability to work well together.

In reality though, Jesus had a clear sense of purpose,[17] and he specifically invited his disciples into that purpose with him. No matter what challenges they faced, Jesus continued to pursue that purpose. That pursuit, however, occurred in the very context of deep relationships where their lives were being formed.

A VISION OF TEAM

Think about a time you were on a great team. Perhaps it was a sports team, a musical ensemble, or some sort of mission or work team. How did it feel? What made it great?

As I coach, I often ask newly-formed teams to describe the characteristics of a high-performing team.[18] Commonly, I hear responses such as trust, shared purpose, team over individual, accomplishes its mission, clearly defined roles, honesty, integrity, strong leadership, synergy, love, commitment, fun, etc. I enjoy seeing the energy level rise during such conversations as people recall their positive experiences. Great teams have qualities that everyone seems to admire and hope to duplicate.

As a sports fan, I am always struck by what happens when championship teams are crowned—I witnessed this recently at the end of an NCAA March Madness tournament. During post-game interviews, you seldom hear players and coaches talk about the game itself. Instead they declare their love for one another, often through tears of joy and laughter. They embrace and jump up and down like little children. Why is this?

Friends, I think it's all about unity! Great teams experience the unity that comes from relationship (love) *and* responsibility/mission (purpose). We were made for this because we are made in the image of God!

This is the vision of team. Mysteriously, it has a glorious quality to it even in a sports team or a musical ensemble. But when team happens like this in a community of Jesus followers, it is deeply transforming and transformative.[19]

Shared leadership (as seen in teams) is the place where relationship and formation are integrated with mission. What if every committee had deep relationships of trust, like the high-performing teams described by those I've coached? How would this affect their decision-making and work? What if every small group had a shared mission together? How would this affect their spiritual growth and friendships? What if we invited people into teams where unity of love *and* purpose were inherently linked together?

I like this definition of team: *Team is where mission and relationship come together, and each team member shares in the responsibility for the team's purpose and outcomes.* Notice the both/and in this definition, as well as the importance of shared responsibility.

Let's break down this both/and.

Relationally—In healthy teams, we are able to focus on our relationship with God and with one another. We are reminded that God is with us and that we do not have to face any of our challenges alone. We are together with God and with one another. We are able to create safe spaces through covenant that can lead to deep, trusting friendships. In the context of these relationships, we are able to hold one another accountable to the convictions that the Spirit brings us in order that we may grow into Christlikeness. We grow to love one another as Christ loves us, and we mirror the interdependence of the Trinity.

Missionally—In a healthy team, we are caught up in a shared calling that is bigger than we are. It is Jesus' mission, and we are invited to participate with God in his work in the world. This work occurs in the context of loving and growing relationships with God and with one another, and we each play our valued part in this shared mission as the Spirit enables us. In other words, we have shared responsibility. This type of Spirit-enabled shared mission over time results in multiplication and leads to a movemental expression.

This is what the both/and unity—that Christ prayed for and that Paul begs us to pursue—looks like in lived form. Woodward and White describe shared leadership in this way:

> *Instead of a solo approach … leadership is shared … it includes a relational group of people who learn to share responsibility, engaging in both leading and following, giving time to be on mission… [It] models the interrelations of the Trinity, an interdependent, communal, relational, participatory, self-surrendering and self-giving approach to leadership… [It] lends itself to a relational approach to leadership, a communal approach to spiritual formation and being the church, an incarnational and distributed approach to mission, and a multiplication approach to movement.[20]*

While the language of team is not in the Bible, this both/and picture of shared leadership can be found throughout the Scriptures. This is what Alan Hirsch describes as *communitas,* where people relate at a deep level resulting from a shared ordeal (walking through an adaptive challenge) in a community formed around a shared purpose.[21]

TYPES OF TEAMS

Remember the definition of team? *Team is where mission and relationship come together, and each team member shares in the responsibility for the team's purpose and outcomes.* With this as a definition, what qualifies as a team?

SLI (Spiritual Leadership, Inc.) describes three types of teams that fit the definition above:

1. **Task teams**—Groups of people who share responsibility to accomplish a task. These teams are often small and exist only as long as it takes to complete the task.

2. **Directional teams**—Provide stakeholder discernment and overall direction for an organization. A typical example of this is a church board. These teams share responsibility and can be a place where both relationship and mission come together. They are often larger teams and typically include representatives from multiple constituencies within an organization. For example, the board or directional team may be made up of a representative from the children's ministry, the youth ministry, the worship ministry, the small group ministry, the outreach ministry, and the finance committee.

3. **Organic teams**—Share responsibility for a particular mission and focus on adaptive leadership.[22] (Note: Both task teams and directional teams primarily focus on technical leadership.)

Each of these teams requires deep relationship and trust. While shared leadership exists in each of these types of teams and each is a legitimate form of team, organic teams are the only ones that multiply over time. The work of task and directional teams is connected to the ongoing and generative work of organic teams. The remainder of this book will primarily focus on the shared leadership necessary for organic teams.

CHARACTERISTICS OF SHARED LEADERSHIP

Back to our jazz band example. In a good ensemble, each of the players brings their own talents and gifts, and each has been honing those gifts through practice. The pattern to the music is known, and they trust one another. As they play, they listen intently to one another, and they take turns soloing and supporting, leading and following. As one improvises, everyone else adjusts so that each person is both executing and learning simultaneously. Each is deferential toward the other players yet courageous to innovate. Each experiences fear of the unknown along with the exhilaration of unexpected surprises. The end result—their performance—impacts and transforms them just as it does their audience. This is an example of shared leadership.[23]

In the previous chapter I described the characteristics and consequences of solo-heroic leadership. In contrast to those, what are the characteristics and holy possibilities of shared leadership? While this list is not exhaustive, here are some key characteristics:

- Shared responsibility
- Loving humility
- High trust, commitment, and accountability
- Collective intelligence
- Adaptive capacity
- Multiplication

SHARED RESPONSIBILITY

I once had the privilege of coaching a pastor from West Virginia, who asked me to help him develop a leadership team around the church's purpose of making disciples. This particular church had been through a failed merger that resulted in broken trust and a disillusioned congregation. The pastor had been serving this congregation for seventeen years and had clear vision for the future. He also held a deep pastoral concern for his people.

As the new team grew in both relational and spiritual depth, the pastor was able to open up about how lonely leadership had been. He described how painful it was, in the church's season of change, to face criticism alone; how much responsibility he had carried by himself. In one particularly transparent moment, he wept as he shared these realities. In response, a team member—knowing the pastor faced harsh comments from a small group of people—offered to stand with him in the times he faced criticism. The joy and relief that pastor experienced was life-changing. It also freed and empowered others around him to step into their giftedness and calling.

This is the joy of shared responsibility! You do not have to lead alone. You are not meant to lead alone. Life, leadership, and ministry are all much better when we have partners in the journey. When there is a community of leadership that shares both love and purpose, what emerges is shared responsibility for the desired outcomes of the organization. Rather than everything resting on the heroics of a solo leader, this paradigm invites camaraderie around shared passion and calling, as well as a division of the work, which makes it more bearable for all.

Shared responsibility can also lead to sharing authority. In a desire for control, the solo-heroic leader clings to their formal position and falls prey to the misperception that sharing authority limits their influence. In contrast to this, many of the most influential and world-changing leaders throughout history held no title and certainly didn't cling to a position as the source of their influence.[24] Healthy spiritual leaders know that their authority comes primarily through relationships and through demonstrating effectiveness over time. They also know that giving away authority to other leaders around them does not decrease their influence but actually increases it over time.

LOVING HUMILITY

Have you ever been led by someone who models true Christlike humility? Someone you know deeply cares for you?

I recently went through a challenging season, and one of my primary mentors exhibited this kind of loving humility toward me. He is a visionary leader and could have simply tried to fix me or rescue me from my situation. Instead, motivated by my good, he set aside whatever agenda he might have had and listened, encouraged, and walked with me. In so doing, he invited me back into being led by the Holy Spirit.

False humility appears to have the best interests of others in mind but is secretly self-serving. True humility, on the other hand, is motivated by love of others, and is expressed through service. This is why true Christlike humility must be linked to Christlike love.

While the desire for control is often accompanied by a desire for power, the humble leader seeks to *empower* others. Jesus understood these same distinctions and was quite specific in his description of the kind of leader that God seeks:

> *"You know that the rulers of the Gentiles lord it over them, and their great ones are tyrants over them. It will not be so among you; but whoever wishes to be great among you must be your servant, and whoever*

*wishes to be first among you must be your slave; just as the Son of Man
came not to be served but to serve, and to give his life a ransom for
many."*

Matthew 20:25b–28

Jesus is clear that seeking power and lording it over others is not the kind of
leadership he desires. The posture of humility and loving service overcomes
the self-referential worldview of the solo-heroic leader that often leads to
narcissism. This posture is the kenosis we discussed in chapter one. Jesus
invites us to the same loving humility that he exhibits.

HIGH TRUST, COMMITMENT, AND ACCOUNTABILITY

A friend of mine was leading a congregation described by one of its lay
leaders as "hard on pastors." This pastor was under constant fire from a small,
insular group that wanted their own way. She believed in the concept of
shared leadership but wasn't sure how to get started. Together, we launched
a team that began to grow spiritually, sought the Lord, and discerned how to
make disciples in their community. Over time, the team grew in trust, as they
held one another accountable to an explicit covenant they co-developed.
They clarified the church's vision and calling, and the team shared a deep
commitment to one another and to that vision. A few months into their
team process, the pastor discovered that some of her team members were
confronting the negativity coming from that insular group. Rather than
facing those battles alone, she now had partners in ministry that were as
committed as she was. Once that negative group realized they had lost their
ability to manipulate and control, it wasn't long before they voluntarily left
the church. The leaders on my friend's team then began launching new teams
and ministries that multiplied the DNA they were experiencing. The result
was a fruitful, life-changing mission into their community.

When there is shared responsibility and leaders exhibit loving humility,
this creates the environment for high trust, commitment, and accountability. Trust typically takes time and intentionality to build, but it is catalyzed
by the vulnerability of a Christlike leader who is motivated by love. When

there is a trusting relationship, there is the potential for deep commitment and accountability to a shared purpose.[25]

The early apostles deeply trusted in God, but they also trusted others as God would lead them. This shared trust led to a deep commitment to Christ and to one another. In other words, they had unity and harmony in their relationships with a deep commitment to one another and to their shared purpose.

When high trust, deep commitment, and intentional accountability is experienced in an environment of shared leadership, what follows is "collective intelligence."

COLLECTIVE INTELLIGENCE

Brian Eno, an English musician and producer, coined the term *scenius* to describe the genius embedded in a *scene* rather than in one's individual *genes*. He describes it this way:

> I was an art student and, like all art students, I was encouraged to believe that there were a few great figures like Picasso and Kandinsky, Rembrandt and Giotto and so on who sort-of appeared out of nowhere and produced artistic revolution. As I looked at art more and more, I discovered that that wasn't really a true picture.
>
> What really happened was that there was sometimes very fertile scenes involving lots and lots of people—some of them artists, some of them collectors, some of them curators, thinkers, theorists, people who were fashionable and knew what the hip things were—all sorts of people who created a kind of ecology of talent. And out of that ecology arose some wonderful work.
>
> The period that I was particularly interested in, 'round about the Russian revolution, shows this extremely well. So I thought that originally those few individuals who'd survived in history—in the sort-of "Great Man" theory of history—they were called "geniuses". But what I thought was interesting was the fact that they all came out of a scene that was very fertile and very intelligent.
>
> So I came up with this word "scenius"—and scenius is the intelligence of a whole ... operation or group of people. And I think that's a more useful

way to think about culture, actually. I think that—let's forget the idea of "genius" for a little while, let's think about the whole ecology of ideas that give rise to good new thoughts and good new work.[26]

Eno's description of scenius is a picture of collective intelligence. When there is shared responsibility in an environment of trust, commitment, and accountability, the collective genius of a team or organization far outweighs the intelligence or gifts of any individual. This synergy means the sum is truly greater than the parts.

Many leaders function under the assumption that if things are to be done right, then the leader will have to get the work done. This fits squarely in the solo-heroic leadership paradigm, in which all meaningful work is built on the intelligence, experience, giftedness, and intuition of those in charge. Any leader who has worked with an effective team sees the fallacy of such a paradigm, because collective intelligence is wiser and more effective than the lone genius. The caveat to this, is that, for this to be the case, there has to be trust, commitment, accountability, shared responsibility, and diversity of gifts and perspectives.

A highly effective leader in a church or other organization who lacks trust and shared responsibility is indeed likely to get more done working alone than s/he would while working in an ineffective team. Many leaders have experienced organizations with dysfunctional teams and groups, and this can lead us to prefer to work alone. Sometimes, leaders understand the benefit of effective teams but believe they don't have the time or the tools necessary to make teams work. Shifting to a shared leadership paradigm does take time and intentional investment, so many leaders opt for the easier route of solo-heroic leadership and perpetuate that paradigm.

When characteristics of shared leadership are in place in a team of leaders with diverse gifts and perspectives, there is no question that the team's capacities far exceed the capacities of a single leader.

ADAPTIVE CAPACITY

Jorge and Wes, who I mentioned in chapter two, have now been leading together in a culture of shared leadership for more than a decade. In their various leadership teams there is tremendous trust, as well as clear diversity of gifts, perspectives, and roles. In the early days of their team leadership, fairly minor adaptive challenges could be overwhelming and tempt them to revert to a solo-heroic model. With each new challenge, though, facing them together in team not only demonstrated the growing collective intelligence of their organization but also increased their ability to live in the tension of adaptive leadership. Having practiced this for many years now, they are able to face even the most complex adaptive challenges with care, discernment, vision, and even joy.

As a team grows in trust and faces greater and greater challenges together, it has the ability to tolerate greater and greater tension. Greater tolerance to tension provides the necessary muscles of creativity to discern solutions. All of this combines to provide the courage to experiment with new learning and build new culture.

MULTIPLICATION

Disciples beget disciples. Spiritual leaders beget spiritual leaders. Effective adaptive leadership teams beget more teams.

The inability of solo-heroic leadership to repeat past success is because everything is built on the back of the leader. In the shared leadership paradigm, each individual is a valued member of the team, yet no single person becomes indispensable. If each person on the team carries the "master" DNA, is equipped into shared spiritual leadership, and is empowered to lead with others, then there exists the seeds of a generative movement.

INVITATION TO ABIDE

Near the end of Jesus' earthly ministry, he walked through a vineyard with his disciples. He reminded them that he is the vine, they are the branches, and his Father is the gardener. He invites them to abide in him even as he abides in them and promises that if they do, they will bear much fruit that will bring the Father glory and prove that they are his disciples. Imagine him picking up a branch from the ground and tossing it into the fire, declaring that apart from him they can do nothing. Then hear the intimacy with which Jesus describes the disciples abiding in his love, in the same way that Jesus abides in the Father's love—and his promise that as they do so they will experience complete joy.[27]

All of the characteristics of shared leadership that we've discussed can be powerful and can bring generative results if built on the right foundations. But, as spiritual leaders, we must remember that we are not the source of that power or that fruitfulness. In countless moments of coaching leaders and churches, I hear the desire to be more fruitful. Sometimes this comes from churches who are already fruitful but want to do better. Often it is from churches who feel stagnant (or have been seeking the wrong kind of fruit) and desire to see fruitfulness again. Fruit, though, comes because of something else. That something else is *abiding*.

What does it mean to abide? When I ask this question of everyday disciples, I often hear responses such as "living in, dwelling, remaining, trusting, staying connected with, depending upon."

Interestingly, this picture that Jesus paints of abiding is not merely describing *individuals* abiding in Jesus. It's the picture of a vineyard, where Jesus is the vine, and *we* are the branches. We are to be abiding in Jesus *together*. This is a communal, corporate picture of abiding that requires us to not only be deeply connected with Jesus but also to be deeply connected to one another. Only in shared abiding can we experience the generative possibilities of fruitful transformation that impacts our world.

PART 2

A FRAMEWORK FOR LEADING TOGETHER

In this second section, we will look more closely at a framework of shared spiritual leadership. In chapter four, this framework focuses on the importance of leading in and with God and doing so through love. In chapter five, this framework focuses on leading together through an adaptive leadership process.

John 15

4

CHANGED BY THE MUSIC: LEADING AS A MEANS OF GRACE

I sat transfixed watching Benjamin Zander work with an amazing young cello player. Technically, she was flawless, but something was missing. While she played beautifully, the piece didn't move me. But, as Zander coached, the cellist got caught up in the music and it transformed the performance. In reflection, she said, "I'd forgotten ... Why did I devote eight hours a day during my entire childhood to practicing this? It wasn't because my mother locked me in a closet. It was because I sat down and couldn't get up *because I loved it so much*. He helped me remember that."

The cellist experienced a shift—a transformation—when she remembered that she is a conduit for the music. And when she was transformed, so was her audience. Zander's leadership became a means for her reorientation. Interestingly, his coaching assumed she already knew how to play the instrument, but at some point she had forgotten *why* she was playing. The means had become the end. The real end was the music itself—the beauty and impact the music could bring in her own life and in the lives of others. She continued, "I'm trying to remember that my barriers don't have to be there. ... I'm not going to stop seeking perfection, but perfection is not to be gained at the cost of music."[1]

What a powerful statement! Just as the beauty of music can be sacrificed on the altar of slaving for technical perfection, the life-changing work of grace in and through us can be sacrificed on the altar of our own self-effort, control, and religious striving.

Two of my heroes of the faith are John and Charles Wesley, who helped lead one of the most remarkable missional movements in church history. Hundreds of years ago, John Wesley reminded the early Methodists of the proper priority of means and ends:

> *In using all means, seek God alone. In and through every outward thing, look only to the power of His Spirit, and the merits of His Son. Beware you do not get stuck in the work itself; if you do, it is all lost labor. Nothing short of God can satisfy your soul. Therefore, fix on Him in all, through all, and above all.*[2]

Notice Wesley's encouragement to use any *means* necessary to seek and serve God but to be careful that the *means* do not distract us or move us away from God alone. Isn't it interesting how easy it is for us to lose sight of the *Giver* and only look for the *gifts?*

These "means" of grace that Wesley refers to are the practices that position us to receive transformative grace and that, as leaders, allow transforming grace to flow through us into the lives of others.[3] In other words, the Holy Spirit utilizes these *means* of grace to grow us to *become* more like Jesus and to *lead* more like Jesus. The power is not in the practices, but in the grace of God. The practices, however, can be a *means* of us receiving and passing along that grace.

We ended the last chapter with the need to abide in Christ individually and corporately. We often think of abiding as a passive surrender; however, true abiding involves active participation—an ongoing, intentional decision to trust God, let go of control, and receive his grace. Our spiritual growth is the work of God in us, and likewise our spiritual leadership must be the work of God in and through us. If it is not rooted in the grace of God, it becomes about us rather than him.

BEAR NOT PRODUCE

So what does leading others and leading together look like as a means of grace?

What is God's part? What is our part? And how does this all work together? What are the postures and practices that are helpful?

The overarching answer may lie in John 15. As I read about the vine and the branches in verses 1–11, I'm always struck that the branches don't *produce* fruit; they *bear* fruit. In a world of production and consumption, many of us are trying to *produce* something, but what does it look like to simply *bear* fruit? Consider the pastor who spends all week working on a sermon but spends little to no time in prayer or communion with God otherwise; trying to produce something *for* God rather than receiving something in relationship *with* God.

I experienced this when I found myself trying to figure out what God might want me to say to an audience, but I was attempting this in my own strength. I felt a strong conviction that I must let God lead me. If I simply worked out something clever to say (producing something for God), then God would not transform lives through it. Instead, I needed my leadership to be an overflow of God's work in me (bearing fruit).

THE CYCLE OF LOVE

As we said in chapter one, jazz musicians master routines. In fact, they cannot function without them. Practicing and mastering those musical routines makes it possible to be an accomplished musician. Frank Barrett reminds us that those routines can be a strength (what he calls "the success factor"), but they can also be limiting. This is precisely what happened to the cellist I described earlier in the chapter. Barrett's advice—both for jazz musicians and for leaders—is full-bodied immersion, where learning and transformation is part of doing. He describes this as an intense involvement of mind, body, emotions, and intuition and not just a cognitive endeavor. In this immersion, there must be an openness to the immediacy of wonder.[4]

When playing jazz, too much structure is trouble, but so is too little structure. The key is having enough structure to branch off and embellish. That is where transformation is experienced—in this intersection of minimal structures that are non-negotiable with the freedom to experiment and respond to the music in the moment.

How can we apply this principle to leadership? I believe it is in ensuring that love is our non-negotiable, our most basic "structure."

I first developed the concept of the "Cycle of Love" to teach at a retreat for middle school students. I wanted to communicate the idea of embodying God's love in a way that could stick, and it has become a pattern for my life. Following our jazz metaphor, this pattern helps me experience the music of heaven, be transformed by it, and share it with others. It helps me ensure, as much as possible, that all I do is God's work rather than *my* work—being *in* and *with* God as opposed to working *for* God.[5] The Cycle of Love provides a rich foundation for leading as a means of grace and has both *personal* implications for spiritual leaders and *corporate* implications for shared spiritual leadership.

Let's break down the Cycle of Love.

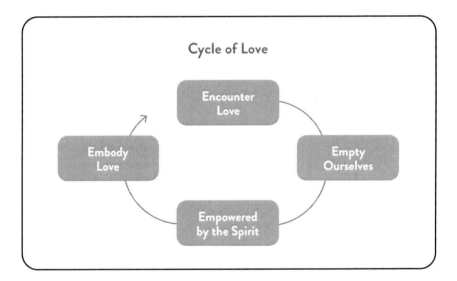

ENCOUNTER LOVE

Most people, even if they are not musicians, love listening to music. What do you love most about it? Why do you enjoy it? How does it make you feel? Music is powerful and often moves us in deep ways. Interestingly, we don't have to *do* anything for this to happen—we simply respond.

In the Cycle of Love, the first phase is to *encounter love*. Everything about us—our identity in Christ, healthy relationships with others, our ministry, our work, our leadership—all begins by encountering love. Daily.

Many Christian leaders are trying to live, love, and lead off yesterday's encounter with God. But just as the manna didn't last for the people of Israel for more than a day,[6] so we can't live our relationship with God and leadership with others from yesterday's provision. When Jesus said, "Abide in me, as I abide in you," he was not referring to a one-time occurrence that we check off the list. It is an *ongoing* journey of abiding. And because everything begins with God, we should live our lives in *response* to him. Whether we are talking about worship, love, prayer, obedience, service, mission, or leadership ... everything is a response to God's love in our lives; a response to encountering the music of the living God of love.

So what does it look like, on a practical level, for followers of Jesus and spiritual leaders to abide deeply in Jesus such that we actually encounter the love of God on a regular basis?

As a start, we go back to the practices Wesley called *means of grace* (such as prayer, searching the Scriptures, fasting, engaging in the Sacraments, being held accountable, etc.). These practices can't simply remain theoretical or theological concepts. Referring to such practices, Dallas Willard said, "The single most obvious trait of those who profess but do not grow into Christ-likeness is their refusal to take the reasonable and time-tested measures for spiritual growth."[7]

I prefer the language of *means of grace* to that of *spiritual disciplines* because it puts the emphasis on the motivation to encounter God in grace. It reminds us that we are utilizing certain practices to better position ourselves to hear and respond to the music of love. While discipline is certainly required, it changes our motivation if the whole purpose of these practices is to encounter the God of love rather than check off some box on a religious to-do list.

I often have a sense that Jesus is waiting for me to wake up in the morning, desiring to abide with me. That thought blows my mind! He is longing to abide with you in the same way.

How do we engage in these and other practices, not to gain God's approval but as an actual means of grace, so that we might tangibly encounter the love of God *every day*? I suppose if this was easy, we'd all be doing it, but clearly it's not! Let me share a little of my own daily rhythm as an example that may prompt ideas for similar practices in your own life.

I read and pray portions of *The Book of Common Prayer*[8] every day. I pray through the Lord's Prayer, using it as an outline to inform my praise, intercession, confession, and supplication. I spend time waiting and listening in silence and solitude to the voice of the Lord. I often journal what I am grateful for and what the Lord is allowing me to see and hear. I spend a great deal of time meditating upon and praying Scripture I have memorized. Dallas Willard said this may be one of the most spiritually formative habits we can practice and is more important than a "daily quiet time."[9] I have found this to be true in my own life. I have also experienced firsthand that becoming Christlike and being a true spiritual leader requires regular accountability in the body of Christ, so I meet weekly with my accountability partner and monthly with my spiritual director. I owe much to mentors who helped form me in these practices, along with many authors and spiritual guides—such as Dallas Willard, N. T. Wright, Richard Foster, Ruth Haley Barton, Robert Mulholland, and Stephen Seamands.

For many followers of Christ, one of the biggest barriers to spending daily time with the Lord is that it feels like an obligation. Others of us know the practice is important, but we allow our busy lives to be an excuse. For still others, the many "digital distractions" in our lives keep us occupied. So how do we overcome these barriers and challenges?

One of the things that helps me most is being reminded that I am both infinitely valuable to God and that God doesn't need me to accomplish his plans for him. This reminder of my value reshapes how I approach God, but it hasn't always been that way. I struggled for many years with a sense of obligation to seek and serve God because of all that Christ had done for me—as if somehow I could earn God's approval, and, by so doing, earn the right for God to use me. But, we are not simply pawns for some distant king to use. We are God's beloved—his children and his friends.[10] *Encountering* God in this way—as one who is deeply loved and valued—has transformed me and continues to do so. I've discovered that I not only need this kind of encounter every day, I also really want it. It is in abiding in God's presence that our deepest human longings for love and belonging are satisfied. This is no longer an obligation but a delight because I am delighted in.

On a practical level, given my own busyness and tendency to be distracted, I treat my time of abiding as the most important appointment on my schedule. I do not pick up technology, open social media, or check the news until after this appointment. While it may feel like there is critical "work" to get done, if I believe Jesus' words in John 15 then I have to trust that I will be fruitful only when I am abiding.

None of the rest of this cycle of love is possible if we don't *encounter* the love of God continually. We are conduits of God's love just as the cellist is a conduit for the music. Whether we are talking about our discipleship or our leadership, love must flow through us. Yesterday's manna, yesterday's *encounter* with God, is not sufficient for today. We must abide in Jesus' love just as he abides in the Father's love, and when we do, we will experience the complete joy of Jesus.[11] This is precisely why we pray that the Lord will give us today our daily bread, both physically and spiritually.[12]

EMPTY OURSELVES   *KENOSIS*

If we want to be transformed by music, we have to listen and let go. I will never be truly moved by a song or piece of music if I am distracted. When I am fully engaged and surrendered to it, listening to music brings me deep joy. The hair on the back of my neck might stand up or tears might fill my eyes.

Similarly, as we encounter the love of God, we are invited to *empty ourselves*, to surrender, to lay ourselves down. We are not emptying ourselves of our identity and calling, but—as in the description of Jesus in Philippians 2—we are emptying ourselves of privilege … of anything and everything that could be exploited for our gain. To empty myself requires the *posture* of humility, but it requires the *practice* of surrender. In Luke 9:23 Jesus said that anyone who wants to be his follower must deny him/herself every day and follow him. This is not about beating yourself up. Instead, it is saying, "Lord, I want to live faithfully to the calling I have received, and I don't want this to be about me today."

My own pattern and practice for this comes from Revelation 4. One of my beloved professors in seminary was Dr. Robert Mulholland. In his course on Revelation, he described the twenty-four elders in chapter four as representative of the church. These elders bow down before the One seated on the throne, worship, and cast their crowns at his feet.[13] It is a three-fold practice: they *bow down*, they *worship*, and they *cast their crowns* (their accomplishments and achievements—anything that is to their credit). I am the kind of person who likes to use my body when I worship and pray. As such, it is part of my own daily practice to bow, to worship, and to "cast my crowns" at Jesus' feet. Doing this reminds me that I need to consider everything loss that is to my profit.[14]

According to Paul, everything that is on my ledger, everything I have, all of my study, my accomplishments, even my lineage, is worth nothing (is "rubbish") in comparison to knowing Christ. Paul chose to lay it all down, and we face the same choice. It's not that we don't have worth, but instead that our infinite worth comes from being made in the image of God. If our accomplishments and gifting become the things from which we draw our identity, then it becomes all about me. When I lay those things down, then I no longer live, but Christ lives in me.[15]

Why is this letting go and emptying ourselves so hard? Think about your life, your influence, your training, your many accomplishments, your failures, your roles, and the positions you hold. These things are all important to us and treating them as insignificant is difficult. I still hold on to my own accomplishments, my education, and my influence as if these things define me. In a society that values what we do over who we are, it is easy to get caught in this trap. Letting go of these things requires me to acknowledge that all my good comes from God alone. It requires me to admit, as difficult as it is for me, that I am not the one in control.

Letting go of my failures is sometimes more difficult for me than letting go of what is to my profit. I often feel as though I should dwell on my failures, as if they are some sort of reminder of how broken I am or as if they somehow more accurately define me. Practically, though, failure is part of every learning process. Why would I think I could live and lead without failing when no one other than Jesus has managed to do it? This is nothing but arrogance. What is more, when my failures are associated with sin in my life (as some of them are), it is also arrogant for me to continue to hold against myself what I have confessed and God has already forgiven.

When I *bow down*, *worship*, and *cast my crowns* at Jesus' feet each day in my times of abiding, I regularly name that God is God and I am not. I rehearse daily the goodness and character of God in worship and adoration. Then I give God back the things he has given me, including my family, my influence, my education, my accomplishments, my roles, and my positions. I *empty myself* in response to God's great love and new mercy for me each day. There is nothing magical about the practice of surrender itself, but it positions me in humility to receive grace.

Without encountering the love of God ourselves, we will not be ready to respond in surrender. So, are you encountering him? Are you abiding in Jesus? If you are, are you able to trust God enough to let go and *empty yourself* of what you have?

EMPOWERED BY THE SPIRIT

Author and psychologist Mihaly Csikszentmihalyi coined the term *flow* to describe the experience of effortless action where we feel no conflicts or contradictions.[16] As Robert Quinn reflects on this state he says, "There is harmony among our feelings, desires, and thoughts. Athletes speak of it as 'being in the zone'; mystics speak of 'ecstasy'; and artists speak of 'rapture.'"[17] Musicians experience *flow* as they are carried along by the music. In chapter three, I described a time where my band was leading a particular song, and I felt as if I was transported to another place and time. This was certainly an experience of *flow*, but it went beyond the music. The Holy Spirit brought the *flow*.

The believers in the book of Acts were filled with the Spirit over and over and over again. I'm struck with how desperately I need that in my life: every single day to be filled with the Spirit, to be *empowered by the Spirit*. Jesus told his disciples to go to the upper room and wait for the Spirit, and that when the Spirit came upon them, they would have power, and they would be his witnesses.[18] This is not merely power to do great things; it is the actual presence of the Spirit in our lives, so that we might be the physical hands and feet of Jesus. For this to be possible, we must receive from the Spirit, which enables us to be continuously transformed. We are not transforming ourselves, and we are certainly not transforming others. We are *being* transformed from one degree of glory to another, and this comes by the Spirit.[19]

The secret sauce of spiritual leadership is this: God living in and through me,[20] whether I'm in my role as a parent, a friend, a leader, a professor, a coach, or a pastor. We encounter the very God of love every day, and in response we empty ourselves in his presence. As we do this, our empty vessel can be filled and empowered by the Holy Spirit and therefore we *bear* the fruit of the Spirit.[21]

Perhaps an analogy is helpful here. In the biblical picture of a vineyard in John 15, Jesus is the vine, the Father is the gardener, and we are the branches. My friend and mentor Ron Crandall expanded this imagery for me to see the Holy Spirit as the "sap" that carries the nutrients of the vine to the branches enabling them to bear fruit.

What does this look like for us in practical terms? How do we give time and attention to allow ourselves to be empowered by the Spirit?

One way is to wait.

Have you ever noticed the number of times we are encouraged or commanded to *wait* on the Lord throughout the grand story of the Bible? As one example, remember the lament of the prophet Jeremiah. He recalls, bitterly, his feelings of utter lostness, pain, and hitting rock bottom. Here's how Eugene Peterson paraphrases Jeremiah's next thoughts:

> But there's one other thing I remember,
> and remembering, I keep a grip on hope:
>
> GOD's loyal love couldn't have run out,
> his merciful love couldn't have dried up.
> They're created new every morning.
> How great your faithfulness!
> I'm sticking with GOD (I say it over and over).
> He's all I've got left.
>
> GOD proves to be good to the man who passionately waits,
> to the woman who diligently seeks.
> It's a good thing to quietly hope,
> quietly hope for help from GOD.
> It's a good thing when you're young
> to stick it out through the hard times.

When life is heavy and hard to take,
go off by yourself. Enter the silence.
Bow in prayer. Don't ask questions:
Wait for hope to appear.
Don't run from trouble. Take it full-face.
The "worst" is never the worst.

Why? Because the Master won't ever
walk out and fail to return.
If he works severely, he also works tenderly.
His stockpiles of loyal love are immense.

Lamentations 3:21–32 MSG

Waiting is hard for me. This is true not only because I struggle to be patient and trust the Lord, but also because I am a doer. I want to get things done. I want to see things change. I want to make a difference. God wants to see things change, too, and wants me to join him in the work of transformation. But I am struck by Moses' prayer in Exodus 33 where he insists that he will not lead the people *unless God's presence will go with them.* Moses knew that it was God's presence alone that made these people distinct from everyone else on the face of the earth.[22] Friends, the same is true for us. It is not our gifts, influence, networks, or authority that makes us distinct—it is God's very presence. This is what we most need.

The early believers in the book of Acts waited for weeks for the promise of the Holy Spirit, and only when the Spirit filled them were they empowered and witnessed to the Risen Lord in transforming ways. Are you waiting in that emptied posture in response to God's great love and faithfulness?

In order for me to wait, I have to find a place of silence, stillness, and solitude. And since I am easily distracted, this must be intentional. I build Sabbath rhythms into each day and each week. Then, once a month, I take a day apart simply for waiting, listening, abiding, journaling, reflecting, and responding. My schedule is such that this will not happen if I do not put it on my calendar. In order to keep me from finding some excuse to forego this most important time of waiting, I intentionally share these things with my accountability partner and report them to my spiritual director.

EMBODY LOVE

Play the music, baby!

Just as fruit exists not to make a tree look pretty but to nourish others, music isn't created to exist on pieces of paper. It is meant to be performed. My friend David says that one of the things he loves most about music is the profoundly relational nature of creating and experiencing it. As he put it, "Bach may have finished scores in 1723, but it is in listening to Yo-Yo Ma play them today that I am deeply moved."

The final stage of this cycle—where we *embody the love of God*—is profoundly relational.

I think of this when I consider the way I want to interact with my family, my friends, and the world. I want to display the fruit of the Spirit (love, joy, peace, patience, kindness, goodness, faithfulness, gentleness, and self-control).[23] But, as a Type-A, get-'r-done kind of person, I have to realize that I can't produce that fruit in my own image, my own strength, my own capacities. The only way we pull it off is to *bear*, not try to *produce*, the fruit of the Spirit.

Take *patience*, for example. I used to think I was patient … until I had children. I've discovered I'm not! Or *gentleness*. I never thought I was an angry person … until I had children. Then I realized I have a lot of anger inside of me, and I'm not sure where it comes from. I talk to my spiritual director about these things, but it is only as I encounter the love of God, as I empty myself of all that is to my profit and all that is to my detriment, as the Spirit fills me, that I am able to embody the very love of God.

Allow me to describe one way I've grown in this area.

For several years as a young parent, I asked my accountability partner to check me on bearing the fruit of the Spirit in my home. Although I was serious about this, I made very little progress. I began to think about what kind of practices could be a *means of grace* for me to encounter God in his love and then to surrender to that love in such a way that I could share it with my family more faithfully. During a sabbatical period, I began to pay attention to my own emotions and to wait on the Lord for what he might want to help me see or hear.[24] As I journaled and continued conversations with a few trusted friends and mentors, I began to identify some "triggers" for my anger. I asked for prayer that I could recognize and name my emotions and even what I was feeling in my body when those emotions would arise. I realized that, prior to getting angry with my kids, I would often grit my teeth and raise my voice. I felt like I was talking more *at* my children than *with* them. I learned to take a deep breath as soon as I felt myself gritting my teeth and emotion building. Breathing acted like a prayer of sorts that allowed me to acknowledge my anger and empty myself with the Lord. As I took that breath, I would kneel and look my children in the eyes and try to ask a question rather than raise my voice in anger. The very act of breathing and kneeling allowed me to submit myself to the Lord and be present with my kids. It is quite difficult for me to raise my voice when I am gazing into their eyes. I don't know how this has affected them, but it certainly has changed me.

Charles Wesley talked of emptying himself of "all but love."[25] However incomplete my love may be at this stage, I long for it to become increasingly complete every day. I still have a long way to go on this journey toward spiritual and emotional maturity, but I share my stories because I assume, as fellow Christ-followers, this is what you desire as well. As we interact with others and lead others, we want our love to be mature and genuine.

Recall again Jesus words in John 15: "Abide in my love, *in the same way, that I abide in the Father's love*" (emphasis mine). Think about that. We're being asked to abide in the love of the Son *in the very same way* that the Son abides in the Father's love. How is that possible? How do we encounter that love? How do we empty ourselves and be filled with God's love that we might embody the fruit of love with others?

Emptying ourselves is all about *humility,* but embodying love is also about *confidence.* This confidence is not in *who* we are but in *whose* we are. This combination of humility *and* confidence may seem paradoxical; yet it is exactly the way Jesus led. It is how many others throughout Scripture led. Leaders we follow out of choice rather than hierarchy also tend to carry those two seemingly opposing markers. They lead with true confidence in who God made them to be and how God has gifted them, as well as deep humility because they know that God is their source.

I think of the cellist that I began this chapter with. She had practiced her entire life. She was clearly gifted by God, and her extensive preparation became a means for her own growth. Her coach, though, reminded her of her *love*, and she found herself in the *flow* of the music that changed not only her life but also the lives of those listening.

To summarize, notice that the Cycle of Love begins with God. We *encounter* God's love and presence, abiding in Jesus as he abides in us, and we respond through letting go as *emptied* vessels, simply *being* in and with Christ. In that emptied state, we are transformed and *empowered* as the Holy Spirit floods us and fills us, making us more like Jesus. When we are filled with the presence and power of the Spirit in this way, the very love of God overflows from us to be poured into the lives of others as we *embody* that love. This overflow spills onto others as we share the gifts that God has given us in the presence and power of the Spirit. Our *being* in Christ leads to our *doing* with Christ in the power of the Spirit to the glory of God.

SPIRITUAL LEADERSHIP IN ACTION

Few people I know more fully embody the Cycle of Love than my wife, MyLinda. She has always said yes to God and, as she has surrendered to Christ, the Holy Spirit consistently empowers her to acts of faith and love.

At one point in our marriage, we had the privilege of serving together as missionaries in Panama where we led a team of young people. One day we were called upon to serve at the Mother Teresa Home, which housed disabled people of all ages. I took the young men in our group to a wing full of men who had various health conditions—some were blind, deaf, or mentally disabled. My wife took the young women to take care of children with similar conditions.

The men's ward was filthy, with urine on the floors and no bedpans. A couple of the young men on my team seemed quite comfortable ministering in these circumstances but, although I felt sorry for the men, I had no idea what to do. Neither did most of the other guys. In my ignorance, I found myself shrinking back from people and hoping the day would end.

Then, I went and joined MyLinda and the young women in the children's ward. It was a jarring experience. I watched in amazement as my wife changed diapers on little babies with no arms and legs. Completely at ease, she ministered with deep compassion. And because she served in this way, the other young women on our team were following her example. In the guy's ward, the men's eyes were filled with fear and anxiety; but in the children's ward, there was no such concern. What was different? In response to God's great love for her, MyLinda had come to the end of herself. In that emptied state, the Holy Spirit empowered her to bear the fruit of love, and it was contagious and transforming.

As you may imagine, serving in this way was not new for MyLinda. It was a natural—or, better said, supernatural—second-nature response for her because she had been practicing this Cycle of Love for years. When she was quite young, she encountered the love of God deeply and personally, which shaped her identity and sense of who God made her to be. She so regularly and consistently emptied herself that it was simply the way she lived—and it still is today. She is selfless and compassionate toward others, which is clearly the *flow* of God's Spirit in and through her. Like the cellist who practiced her entire life, MyLinda has practiced this pattern, and when the Spirit moves in her, the music of love she plays is profound and transforming. I get to experience it regularly. I am the man I am today due not in small part to her love—because her love is God's love for me.

A LIFE OF LOVE

What are the implications of the Cycle of Love as we think about shared spiritual leadership? At the beginning of Ephesians 5, we are urged to live a life of love, just as Christ loved us and gave himself up for us.[26] Even as we resonate with this, it's incredibly challenging to think about loving as God loves us in Christ—*loving just like Jesus*. When I put my life next to Jesus, side by side, there's a big gap!

One of the exercises I do in SLI's Spiritual Leadership Generator[27] (developing lay leaders in local churches) is to have each person take one page of a journal and write out their sense of calling. People articulate their call beautifully. Next, I then ask them to write everything they can to describe Jesus. It doesn't take long to fill up a page. And it's all great stuff! Finally, on an adjoining page, I ask them to write everything they can think about that describes themselves. It is amazing to me how many Christian leaders who have been discipled in the local church can only reference their shame and inadequacies. No doubt, if given a similar task, many of us would do the same. The beauty of the grace of God, though, is that we are *being transformed* by the Spirit. Those old descriptions don't have to be true anymore. That is precisely why I must die to myself. It is precisely why I need the Spirit to fill me every single day. It is precisely why I want to embody love for others—whether my family, my friends, my neighbors, my students.

As Jesus talks about a life of love, note how many times he connects it to obedience. This is not obligation, but overflow: "If you love me, you will obey" (John 14:14). Obedience is a natural consequence of love, which in this passage is linked specifically to the promised Holy Spirit.[28] Remember that love is the fruit of the Spirit.[29] We follow the One we love as we are empowered by the Spirit. We are obedient. We bear fruit. That's what he's called us to.

It would be easy to assume this journey with Jesus is solitary. Yet, this process or cycle, no matter how you describe it, can only happen within the context of *community*. I can't do this myself. It must be *shared* spiritual leadership. When Jesus said, "I am the Vine, you are the branch*es*" (emphasis mine), though he is talking to me individually, the metaphor —the calling that *we* would be a vineyard—is plural. I can only bear so much fruit by myself; but *together*, if we bear the fruit of love, joy, peace, and patience, we can change the world.

What I know to be true is this: if I don't follow this Cycle of Love, I don't get to play—I don't get to participate with all of you who are also called to embody love. But if we do it *together*, we will bear the fruit of love, and in the process, we will be transformed. We will be a symphony of fruitfulness with rich harmonies rather than just a single instrument playing a melody.

THE HOLY POSSIBILITY OF SPIRITUAL LEADERSHIP

God has called us to participate with him to embody the very love of God with others. This is the holy possibility of spiritual leadership.

Jesus constantly pulled away to abide in the Father's love, to listen to the Father's voice. He said, "I don't do a thing, unless the Father shows me." "I don't say a thing, unless the Father tells me."[30] He chose to abide and empty himself. He was filled with the Spirit and embodied the very love of God with others. This is the pattern we are called to follow.

Becoming a true disciple of Jesus and a true spiritual leader is an iterative (constantly repeating) process in grace that over time simply becomes part of us. In his book *After We Believe,* N. T. Wright describes how living Christlike virtues in grace (empowered by the Spirit) is fundamental to our mission and witness in the world. He reminds us that "faith, hope, and love, the full fruit of the Spirit and the unity of the one body—these were further gifts, available only by the grace of Jesus Christ."[31] Among these virtues, love is primary—the love of God and the love of others. These virtues come in our lives as we "put off" the old and "put on" the new.[32] Only in grace can we embody this kind of love, and the resources the Spirit uses to bring this about in us include prayer, searching the Scriptures, relationships in community, and other repeated practices, which we will look at in more detail in chapter six.

Jesus, along with the New Testament writers, had a vision of people becoming Christlike and participating in the kingdom of God on this side of heaven. If this is what Jesus desires, and the Holy Spirit is the true change agent, how then shall we live with others as spiritual leaders? In the next chapter, we will look at a framework for shared spiritual leadership, then we will move into the third part of the book where we look at how we embody these principles and practices as we face adaptive challenges together.

5

DISSONANCE, HARMONY, AND POSSIBILITY: THE FROM-THROUGH-TO MOVEMENT

We all face so many complex situations that it's easy to become overwhelmed. As an idealist, some of these challenges keep me up at night. I'm haunted by questions, such as:

- How do we reach people who are far from Christ?
- How do we embody and present the gospel in ways that are compelling to younger generations?
- How do we mobilize everyday followers of Jesus into mission?
- What do we do about poverty?
- How do we overcome systemic racism?
- What do we do when hit by a pandemic that completely changes our approach to being the church? *— what did our church do that followed this Book's outline?*

No doubt you have your own list of seemingly unanswerable questions. How will we face these situations? One thing I know is this: It is impossible for one leader alone to have all the answers for these kinds of challenges.

I also know that God is not intimidated by these things. If followers of Jesus are truly abiding in him together, it is possible for us to get above the chaos of our circumstances and see with the Spirit's eyes. We can identify the *holy* possibilities that our greatest disruptions and challenges present for us, and be enabled to move into new frontiers. We can engage in adaptive leadership.

Our natural response to difficult circumstances—what Heifetz, Grashow, and Linksy call *adaptive tension*—is usually less faith-filled. They cite three familiar but ineffective responses:

- do nothing;
- react by flight or fight; or
- look to authority.[1]

In contrast, these authors use a musical metaphor—*orchestrating* conflict—to discuss the positive effect that adaptive tension can provide for us:

> We borrow the term orchestration from music because of the way composers approach the uses of dissonance and consonance in the creation of harmony. Composers treat dissonance as an essential component of harmony. Very few pieces of music or kinds of music use only sounds that are consonant with one another, like Gregorian chant. Using only consonant sounds gives music a timeless, motionless feel to it. Dissonance creates tension in the music, causing the listener to naturally want some kind of resolution. Composers know this, so they put two or more dissonant notes together that do not sound quite right, and then they create different kinds of resolutions to the tension by putting together consonant tones that do sound right. To a composer, the art of harmony is the creative uses of dissonance and consonance, woven together to create tension, a sense of forward motion, resolution, and then tension again until, usually, there is a final resolution.[2]

This brings to mind one of my own musical experiences. As a college student, I had the privilege of singing in the university choir at West Texas A&M University under the direction of Dr. George Biffle. We showed up to rehearsal one day and attempted to sight-read a piece entitled "The Dalliance of the Eagles" by Norman Dello Joio. We all hated it! It was the most challenging piece of music any of us had seen. Dr. Biffle knew we could sing it, but he also knew it would be hard for us. The piece was full of dissonance and complex harmonies that demanded deeper listening to one another and more concentration than we were used to. It seemed like we had rehearsed for weeks before the piece even began to sound like music. Then something shifted. All the listening and practice transformed what had been an awful ordeal with an unusual song into a remarkable experience of synergy, harmony, and beauty. I still remember our public performance. The seats were full, and we were nervous about how the song would be received. The power and beauty of the dissonance and resolution embedded in strategic crescendos and decrescendos resulted in a standing ovation! To this day, it is one of my favorite memories of *sounding together* with others.

Composers such as Dello Joio understand the power of dissonance. As spiritual leaders, how do we capitalize on the tension or dissonance that is present in our circumstances to *orchestrate* learning, growth, experimentation, and ultimately to create something of kingdom beauty? This is key to overcoming challenges and moving into new realities. People already feel the tension, but it is common for us to ignore it or stay busy on easier things (*do nothing*); to fight against it or run from it (*react by flight or fight*); or simply to hope that those "above" us in the organization will fix it (*look to authority*).

THE PERILS OF ADAPTIVE CHANGE

Moving into adaptive leadership can be fraught with danger. In their book *Leadership on the Line*, Heifetz and Linsky say, "Leadership would be a safe undertaking if your organizations and communities only faced problems for which they already knew the solutions."[3] While there may be known solutions to our *technical* challenges, our *adaptive* challenges require experimentation and new learning, which often leads to changing our attitudes, behaviors, and even our values. As Heifetz and Linsky point out, "The sustainability of change depends on having the people with the problem internalize the change itself."[4] They go on to say,

> *People cannot see at the beginning of the adaptive process that the new situation will be any better than the current condition. What they do see clearly is the potential for loss .... When fears and passions run high, people can become desperate as they look to authorities for the answers. This dynamic renders adaptive contexts inherently dangerous.* [5]

When we face the perils of adaptive change, rather than taking the road of Christ, of humility, we often take the road of self-sufficiency, assuming we can lead the change. In fact, there is often a sense of expectation that, as a leader, we're supposed to have the answers. But this is clearly impossible if the world around us is changing. As already stated, it is impossible for one leader to have all the answers for new and complex situations.

As we face adaptive challenges with courage, we will encounter resistance. In his book *A Failure of Nerve,* Edwin Friedman points out that resistance is a systemic phenomenon always associated with leadership and typically indicates that leaders are moving in the right direction.[6] This is true because people have a fear of the unknown and a fear of loss. Heifetz and Linsky say, "In fact, there's a proportionate relationship between risk and adaptive change: The deeper the change and the greater the amount of new learning required, the more resistance there will be and, thus, the greater the danger to those who lead."[7]

In the 2018 movie *Robin Hood,* Robin returns home from the Crusades only to discover that he has been declared dead by the Sheriff of Nottingham so that his land and wealth can be seized for use by the corrupt Cardinal.[8] The commoners are being persecuted unjustly, and, to top it all off, his love Marion is now with another man. He has no way to face the mounting challenges, both personal and communal. At rock-bottom and alone, Robin Hood is confronted by Little John, who recognizes that they need each other if they are to overcome the difficulties they face. John challenges Robin to join forces and fight injustice together. Eventually, alongside Marion and the townspeople, they lead a revolution and surrender themselves on behalf of the people. With both deep humility and bold courage, they overcome what seemed to be insurmountable odds to solve their greatest adaptive challenges.

A CASE STUDY: COMMUNITY OF GRACE

I once worked with several churches that found themselves ministering in a declining community. Their neighborhood had changed dramatically, and the people in these churches were very different from those in their area. They had lost sight of both their mission and vision and were not serving their community. People were not being discipled either inside or outside the church. They were stuck, and their greatest adaptive challenge was to learn how to be the church in a radically changed context.

Three of these congregations decided to close their doors and open as a new church plant called Community of Grace. *Together* they became adaptive spiritual leaders. Now, lives are being transformed, values are being embodied, vision is being reached, and a community is being changed because a set of people were willing to be transformed themselves.[9] The people of Community of Grace, led by God, started with a challenging situation, went through a pain barrier together, and eventually found themselves in a new reality. In the coming pages, I will describe a framework for adaptive leadership, as well as some key implications of shared spiritual leadership that draw on this story.

These three congregations had already tried the solo-heroic leadership paradigm hoping that an extraordinary leader would rescue them from their despair and decline. They had fallen prey to the dangers that Heifetz and Linsky describe. By the time they called for help, they recognized that *they* would have to be the ones to change. They also knew there was no guarantee that trying something new would bring about different results, but they felt compelled to try.

A handful of folks in this new plant—a remnant of sorts—had been praying and were longing for the kingdom of God to show up on earth as it is in heaven. They wanted to impact their community. They wanted to move beyond merely trying to survive. They wanted to see a difference and to make disciples.

They were ready to get started with a change process. I had the great honor, along with another colleague, of helping them build a team of spiritual leaders who created an environment in which adaptive leadership could thrive. We also engaged them in a process that required them to go *through* the dangers rather than avoiding them.

FROM-THROUGH-TO

One of the ways I like to describe the process of adaptive leadership is by using a pattern first described to me by my friend and colleague Dr. Steve

Martyn. He discovered this pattern in the life and writings of Adrian van Kaam, the Roman Catholic priest under whom Steve studied for four years at Duquesne University. It is known as the *from-through-to* movement, and it highlights how the Holy Spirit seeks to work in individuals and organizations, particularly as they face adaptive challenges. In this section we will look first at how this movement is applied to facing personal adaptive challenges, then we will apply them to a larger adaptive leadership process for teams and organizations.

We see this *from-through-to* pattern in Scripture. One example is the Hebrews' journey *from* slavery in Egypt *through* the wilderness *to* the Promised Land. Most of us would have preferred to go immediately *from* slavery *to* the Promised Land, but that is not the way God chooses to work. The wilderness, as it turns out, offers the most potential for transformation, though it is also the place most fraught with danger. Even Jesus experienced the wilderness as he prepared for his public ministry to begin. The writer of Hebrews describes this journey for Jesus and exhorts us to follow our Savior's example:

> *Therefore, since we are surrounded by such a great cloud of witnesses, let us throw off everything that hinders and the sin that so easily entangles. And let us run with perseverance the race marked out for us, fixing our eyes on Jesus, the pioneer and perfecter of faith. For the joy set before him he endured the cross, scorning its shame, and sat down at the right hand of the throne of God. Consider him who endured such opposition from sinners, so that you will not grow weary and lose heart.*

Hebrews 12:1–3 NIV

Notice that at the beginning of his ministry (*from*), Jesus could already see the joy that was to come (*to*), but he had to endure the scorn, shame, and suffering of the cross (*through*) in order for that joy to become reality. In the same way, as followers of Jesus, we too are encouraged to persevere *through* suffering. Read James's words with this *from-through-to* movement in mind:

Consider it pure joy, my brothers and sisters, whenever you face trials of many kinds, because you know that the testing of your faith produces perseverance. Let perseverance finish its work so that you may be mature and complete, not lacking anything.

James 1:2–4 NIV

We are not yet what we will become. While God is seldom the author of our "trials of many kinds," God uses these experiences to bring us to maturity if we persevere.

Or listen to Paul's similar challenge and encouragement:

Therefore, since we are justified by faith, we have peace with God through our Lord Jesus Christ, through whom we have obtained access to this grace in which we stand; and we boast in our hope of sharing the glory of God. And not only that, but we also boast in our sufferings, knowing that suffering produces endurance, and endurance produces character, and character produces hope, and hope does not disappoint us, because God's love has been poured into our hearts through the Holy Spirit that has been given to us.

Romans 5:1–5

As Paul notes (and as we discussed in the previous chapter), what makes this journey *through* suffering possible is the grace in which we now stand. We can endure suffering because we have the hope of sharing the glory of God. As we endure suffering, the Spirit grows the character of Christ in us and leads us into sure hope. We are assured because of the very love of God that the Spirit pours into our hearts. In other words, the Spirit takes us *from* where we are, *through* the challenges we face in life by means of endurance, *to* the character and hope of Christ.

Our human inclination is to stick with what we know—to stay in a comfortable place. We tend to avoid change, even when we know we need it. Why is this? As Chip and Dan Heath point out in their book, *Switch*, "The unavoidable conclusion is this: your brain isn't of one mind."[10] Utilizing an analogy by University of Virginia psychologist Jonathan Haidt,[11] the Heath brothers describe the emotional side of us as an Elephant and our rational side as its Rider. Here is how they describe the internal tension we experience when facing change:

> *Perched atop the Elephant, the Rider holds the reins and seems to be the leader. But the Rider's control is precarious because the Rider is so small relative to the Elephant. Anytime the six-ton Elephant and the Rider disagree about which direction to go, the Rider is going to lose. He's completely overmatched.*[12]

When we get overwhelmed and anxious, the Elephant tends to take over. This is true personally, but it is also true within teams and organizations facing challenges. To overcome this, the Heath brothers recommend *directing* the Rider and *motivating* the Elephant:

> *If you reach the Riders of your team but not the Elephants, team members will have understanding without motivation. If you reach the Elephants but not their Riders, they'll have passion without direction. In both cases, the flaws can be paralyzing. A reluctant Elephant and a wheel-spinning Rider can both ensure that nothing changes. But when Elephants and Riders move together, change can come easily.*[13]

If we have clarity of direction and passion to move in that direction, we can move *from* where we are, *through* our challenges, *to* the place where we are being called. This is why tension and disruption can be so beneficial for us. They are the dissonance that demand a resolution. We don't naturally seek out from-through-to movement; an external factor will often compel us, such as frustration or pain that comes from our current reality or the beauty and holy possibility of the prize on the other side of change. Either way, the Holy Spirit uses this motivator to keep us moving *through*. The Promised Land motivated the Israelites to journey—and their forty years in the wilderness is a case in point of what happens when we resist the *through* process. For Jesus, it was "the joy set before him" that motivated him to push *through*.

What does the *through* look like for us? What might we have to stop, start, or surrender in order to go *through*? Do we have a clear calling or direction that keeps us moving *through* even when things get hard?

AN ADAPTIVE LEADERSHIP PROCESS

It is easy to see the application to leadership of this *from-through-to* movement. I once had the privilege of hearing Dr. Henry Cloud speak at a Catalyst Conference in Lexington, Kentucky. The definition of leadership he used that day is the simplest and most helpful I've heard: "Leadership is helping people get *from* here *to* there." In order to get *from* here *to* there, we cannot skirt around our challenges, and we certainly cannot ignore them. We must go *through* them. This is the process or pathway of change, and God is the one who leads us *through* it.

Hear the words of the Psalmist and reflect on how God leads us *through:*

In the day of my trouble I seek the Lord, …
I am so troubled that I cannot speak. …

"Has God forgotten to be gracious?
Has he in anger shut up his compassion?"

I will call to mind the deeds of the Lord; …
I will remember your wonders of old.
Your way, O God, is holy.
What god is so great as our God? …
When the waters saw you, O God,
when the waters saw you, they were afraid;
the very deep trembled. …
Your way was through *the sea,*
your path, through *the mighty waters;*
yet your footprints were unseen.
You led your people like a flock.

Psalm 77, emphasis mine

Do we trust the Lord to lead us *through* our greatest challenges? Is there a process we can follow that will help us discern our way *through*? I submit there is.

PRE-CHANGE (*FROM*)

As we said when considering dissonance, in any place you lead there is probably some form of adaptive tension at play. (See Diagram 1.) It likely has nothing to do with your leadership but simply preexists, creating the possibility—maybe even the urgency—for change. This tension could be associated with pain from the past or it might merely arise from a hope for a better future. It will often disrupt the equilibrium and cause you and your people to feel as if they are at the "edge of chaos."

These pre-change dynamics (*from*) highlight the need for adaptive leadership (*through*) in order to get to a new reality (*to*).

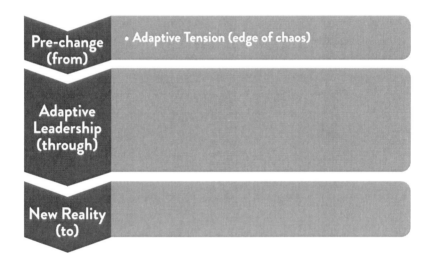

Diagram 1

The three congregations that eventually became Community of Grace were certainly experiencing this "edge of chaos" state. They were in decline and on their way to closure if something didn't change. They didn't want to close, so their resistance to radical change had waned. To put it another way, because of the tremendous dissonance, they were longing for some sort of resolution.

When facing this kind of adaptive tension, most leaders feel compelled to eliminate the chaos to bring about equilibrium and make people feel safe. They fail to realize that this tension or dissonance is the very catalyst that is needed to bring about change and growth. On a personal level, tension usually either leads to greater stress and anxiety, as evidenced by the number of stress-related illnesses, *or* to a willingness to try something new. The same is true for organizations. If we are to capitalize on this adaptive tension, we must create safe relational environments that enable us to live on this edge of chaos.[14]

In chapter seven, we will explore how creating environments is a key role for leaders who are facilitating adaptive change. For now, think about what tension or dissonance is present in your context and how it might open creative and holy possibilities.

ADAPTIVE LEADERSHIP (*THROUGH*)

As we embrace adaptive tension, we move into what is often referred to as *liminal space*.[15] African rites of passage are based on this kind of liminality. Boys, who lived as children with the women in the village, are sent into the jungle together. If they survive, they only do so together, and they return as men. Then they spend the rest of their lives recounting the stories of the shared ordeal of their liminal experience in that "space between."

Many of us may describe the season beginning in early 2020 as liminal space as the world faced the COVID-19 pandemic. In the early stages of the pandemic, Praxis—in partnership with the Murdock Trust—presented a webinar entitled "Strategies for Winter."[16] In it, hosts Andy Crouch and Dave Blanchard debated whether we were facing "a blizzard that might be difficult but would soon pass," or whether the pandemic was actually more like a "long winter." They argued that the more apt metaphor was indeed the long winter and that what would emerge on the other side of the pandemic would be unlike the world we knew before.

One key characteristic of liminality is disorientation. It can feel like everything we have known and relied upon is gone. Those experiencing a shared ordeal, however, move from being disoriented and individualistic to a deep bond of community forged in the fire and tension of liminality. Turner referred to this deep camaraderie as *communitas,* and Hirsch picked up on this dynamic of *liminality* and *communitas* as one of the key components of mDNA necessary for a multiplying movement within the early church.[17]

Community of Grace entered this liminal space as they asked for coaching and agreed to sell everything they owned (putting the church buildings on the market). They committed themselves to the adaptive leadership process, and there was no turning back.

Once we are in this liminal "space between"—where we are no longer where we once were, but we are also not yet where we are going to be—we enter the *through* stage of adaptive leadership. (See Diagram 2.) This stage begins with *increased interaction* among those sharing the challenges, because only *together* will solutions be discovered. Rather than looking to a solo-heroic leader, those affected need to move toward one another. At Community of Grace, this increased interaction first took the form of building deep relationships.

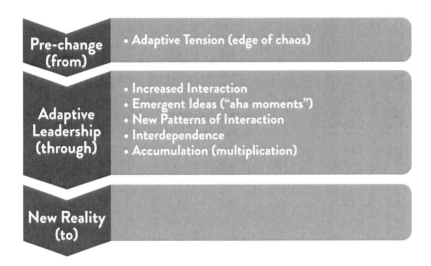

Diagram 2

SLI begins this increased interaction phase of the adaptive leadership process with spiritual formation. The new believers in Acts 2 intentionally lived into the means of grace (devoting themselves to the apostles' teaching, fellowship, the breaking of bread, and the prayers) and, as a result, many were added to their number daily.[18] That is precisely what we invited our friends to embody at Community of Grace. They began hosting a series of concerts of prayer[19] where the three former congregations prayed for one another and for their community. After this initial step, we formed an organic leadership team and got people into accountable relationships with one another. We intentionally created a culture of "loving, learning, and leading"[20] (which I will describe in more detail in later chapters). For many of the team members, these interactions were their first experience of being accountable for what it means to truly follow Jesus.

Marsha, an older woman on the team, shared with me the heartbreaking reality that, despite being in the church for more than seventy years, she had never before been asked about her relationship with Jesus. She also told us that she was unaware she had any responsibility in disciple-making. She assumed this was the work of the pastor and more generally of "the church." During this process, she discovered she is called to be a disciple-maker, and now everywhere Marsha goes, people's lives are being transformed.

The loving, learning, leading emphasis of SLI coaching frames not only our format for meeting but also the kind of culture we are attempting to create. We want to make sure we are discerning together, both with the Holy Spirit and one another, and not merely coming up with our own ideas.[21] As we discern, we often experience "aha moments" when *emergent ideas* arise. Because the Spirit is leading us, these "ahas" go from possibilities to *holy* possibilities. (I find it comical that secular theorists use the language of "aha moments"—as if even *they* don't know how to describe what's occurring! It sounds like the work of grace to me.)

At Community of Grace, the new team began to grow spiritually with one another but also in their trust of God and each other. Their "aha moments" came as they began to imagine what it would look like for the kingdom of God to break into their community.

We can lean into "aha moments" by asking ourselves powerful questions, such as: *What if the God who is able to do immeasurably more than we can ask or imagine*[22] *actually shows up? How does that change our lives, our churches, our community, and our world?* Not only did the team begin to dream, but they also captured those dreams. One woman, who many would not have considered a leader because of her quiet demeanor, described a literal dream she had one night about a church building without walls. From that, a vision began to emerge of what it would be like to be a church without walls. Along with the "ahas" around this emerging vision, the team gained considerable new learning regarding their own values, clarity about their purpose as a church, and their eyes were opened to a sharper picture of their context, both inside the church and in their community.[23]

Over time, this process led to *new patterns of interaction*, which allowed for their learning to multiply and spread through their relationships. At Community of Grace, one of their new patterns of interaction occurred through *covenant groups*. As a team, leaders experienced personal transformation by being held accountable for spiritual growth. This experience was new for them, and they hoped it would be as transformational for others as it had been for them. So, they utilized this same pattern in a variety of ways in their congregation and community to create covenantal groups. Some were small groups that took on this new emphasis, but others were groups with a specific focus, such as the choir, outreach groups, or fellowship groups that now had a covenantal character. There was even a group of men who began to hold one another accountable for spiritual growth when they met to bowl.

The increased interaction, emergent learning, and new patterns of meeting helped create the environment for *interdependence*—an essential phase if we are to move *through* liminality *to* a new reality. This is the *communitas* that we discussed earlier (the realization that we can only overcome adaptive challenges together). Profoundly, people experience genuine joy as they discover the beauty of being the body of Christ together and living into the unity Christ desires for us.[24] In this interdependence, it becomes virtually impossible to name where ideas come from because of the synergy and dynamic nature of team participation. (As in, "It seemed good to the Holy Spirit and to us."[25]) Over time, as we learn more and more, we become more interdependent, and our learning *accumulates*.

Our SLI coaching provided an environment and process for Community of Grace to discern God's direction, but they were the ones doing the work. They were intentionally growing spiritually. They were the ones hearing God's voice and discerning together. As they dreamed God's dreams, they also began to discern what God wanted for their new church and their community. They looked at their own strengths and weaknesses and assessed how they were doing in terms of disciple-making. The more they interacted with the Spirit and one another, the more they learned and discerned, and the more they practiced their learning, the more that learning continued to grow and *accumulate*. In the process, they experienced unity and oneness and were no longer independent but interdependent. This is both the harmony and synergy of shared spiritual leadership. The result: new life was born.

NEW REALITY (*TO*)

By the end of the *through* process, we realize that we have arrived at a completely new reality. This is referred to as *phase transition* because something dramatic has changed. (See Diagram 3.) What happens to water at 32 degrees Fahrenheit is a phase transition. A whole new reality emerges as a liquid becomes a solid. The founders of Community of Grace, *together,* became adaptive spiritual leaders. Their personal and corporate transformation led to transformation in others within their new church and their community. Their values are now articulated, embedded, and embodied in their culture, and they are moving faithfully toward the vision that the Lord planted in them. They moved *from* their very real challenges, *through* personal and corporate change, *to* a new and fruitful reality.

Clearly, this is not an easy process. (Think again of the Hebrew people and a whole generation dying off in the wilderness before they were able to enter the Promised Land.) The sacrifices are immense, and, even once in the new reality, challenges continue, although they are often of a different variety.

While *simple patterns* may emerge to get us through the complexities, it is rarely easy to continue such patterns. The best patterns of interaction to lead us to a new reality ensure that

- Jesus is Lord;
- we are intentional about making disciples;
- our impulses are moving us incarnationally into mission with others;
- we are leading together in ways that look like Jesus and express the fullness of the giftings inherent within the unity of the body of Christ;
- we are at home in liminality and functioning in interdependence; and
- we experience organic and generative multiplication in our community.[26]

As Alan Hirsch points out, if we can establish these patterns, we are likely to experience a multiplying movement. Then, we want to discover how we continue to live together into movement in that new order.

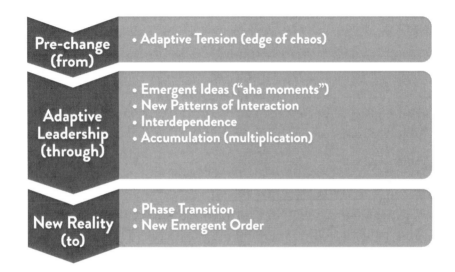

Diagram 3

KEY IMPLICATIONS

We will walk through how to apply this *from-through-to* adaptive spiritual leadership process throughout the remainder of this book, but for now, let's summarize the key implications.

First, as in music—and contrary to what most of us were taught about leadership—dissonance is actually our friend. *Tension is key.* It is the catalyst for change. When faced with adaptive challenges, we can identify tensions and lean in, instead of running away from them. Tension is the dissonance that can lead to beautiful music.

Second, *team is required.* If the leader doesn't know what to do, creating an environment where we can interact around our challenges and learn and grow together (shared leadership) brings about *team leadership.* New patterns emerge as we work on challenges through dynamic interaction. Here we are sounding together.

Third, we want to *learn together* in a way that leads to *interdependence*—like a vineyard, where every branch is interdependent and connected. Not codependence (I can't function without you) but interdependence (I am not meant to live without you). This is unity and harmony.

Finally, as we journey through the process of adaptive leadership—even in highly complex situations—we *identify simple patterns* so that we can *reproduce them*. My friends at Community of Grace discovered patterns that they reproduced in a variety of contexts that led to multiplying transformation in their church and community. These patterns are often discovered by answering some powerful questions, which we will look at in more detail later.

In the end, all of these key implications are built upon the assumption that God alone leads the process of transformation in grace through his Holy Spirit. We are simply participating and leading with God and one another as a means of grace.

TENSION	Tension is key (adaptive challenges)
TEAM	Team leadership (dynamic interaction)
LEARNING	Learning together (interdependence)
PATTERNS	Recognize simple patterns (reproduction)

THE ROLE OF ADAPTIVE SPIRITUAL LEADERS

What is the role of leaders within this process? First, we must *become spiritual leaders who personally model deep change*.[27] This is not about getting other people to change; this is humbly saying, "God change me." It is embodying all that God has called me to and remembering that transformation begins and ends with God (see the Cycle of Love in the previous chapter). Second, we want to *create transforming environments*—to foster the conditions in which change can occur. In this covenantal environment we all embody who God has called us to be and what God has called us to do together. This acknowledges that we don't change anyone, but we do have the ability to shape environments where the Spirit can bring change. Finally, leaders *develop fruitful processes of change.* We are not only shepherding people, but we are also guiding the process in such a way that we keep learning and keep moving and keep growing. This requires discernment; we must understand our current reality (*from*), see and hear what God is leading us toward (*to*), and courageously move *through* our adaptive challenges to become all God has called us to be and do.

Key Principles of Shared Spiritual Leadership

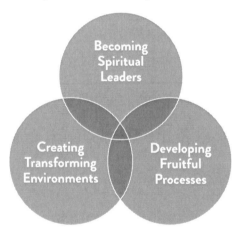

In engaging this way, adaptive leadership becomes shared spiritual leadership.

Consider this an invitation to view leadership in a different way: making sure we are being led by the Spirit and that Jesus is central to all we do; leading in community and not by ourselves; and trusting that the fruit we bear is the very fruit of the Spirit.

In the next section, we shift from a discussion about framework to a more detailed look at the three-part role we play as leaders in this adaptive leadership process. May we become the kind of leaders who embody the very character of Christ Jesus as we lead together.

PART 3

PRINCIPLES AND PRACTICES OF SHARED SPIRITUAL LEADERSHIP

In part one and part two of this book, we've focused on the paradigm and framework of shared spiritual leadership. The hope is that moving in the direction of shared leadership will help us overcome our greatest adaptive challenges and become more fruitful in our mission as Jesus' followers.

Now we move into principles and practices.

As the iceberg image below illustrates, fruitfulness is the ultimate *outcome;* it is what people will see above the surface. *Principles* are the fundamental convictions and beliefs we hold dear that are deep beneath the surface. It is not enough, though, to have strong beliefs and convictions; we must put those principles into action through intentional *practices* if we are to see fruitfulness. These practices are a means of grace that help us engage with God together and remain in the flow of the Spirit's transformation.

Outcomes
A consequence, effect,
or result of something

Practices
A series of actions or steps taken
in order to achieve a particular end

Principles
A fundamental truth or proposition that
serves as the foundation for a system of belief,
behaviors, or a chain of reasoning

The next three chapters will focus on three key principles of shared spiritual leadership and the corresponding practices that support them. In chapter six, we will look at becoming spiritual leaders. Chapter seven will focus on creating transforming environments. And finally, in chapter eight, we will look at developing processes that encourage fruitfulness.

We begin by exploring what it means to become the kind of leaders who embody the very character of Christ Jesus as we lead together.

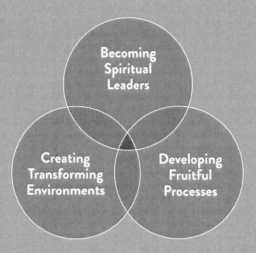

6

MIMICKING THE MASTER: BECOMING A SPIRITUAL LEADER

A number of years ago, while serving as a missionary in India, I had the great joy of helping to lead a ministry conference. The entire experience was amazing, but I was particularly struck by the behavior of a three-year-old boy who was the son of one of the pastors. Even in the high temperatures, he wore a three-piece suit to each session … just like his daddy. During the times of sung worship, the little guy would close his eyes, raise his hands, and sing along … just like his daddy. It was clear he was deeply worshiping the Lord. It was also clear he was imitating his daddy and other spiritual leaders in his environment.

As disciples of Jesus, we all imitate others. In the same way I learned to play jazz by listening to and mimicking the great bassist Abraham Laboriel, we all have people in our lives from whom we have learned what it means to follow Jesus.

Jesus modeled spiritual leadership to all of his disciples, but in this chapter I want to particularly consider his relationship with Peter. As they navigated life together, Jesus developed Peter into a spiritual leader. Peter learned by imitating Jesus.

Imagine yourself in Peter's shoes as I attempt to describe one of his experiences from his perspective.

I used to fish for a living. All that changed when I started following Jesus. He took me and a few others on a great adventure. It was the best time of my life … until a few weeks ago, when I messed it all up.

So, today I decided to go back to what I'm best at: fishing.

A few fisher-friends came with me, and we worked all night. Seems I don't even know how to fish anymore. We didn't catch a thing.

Then, as the sun rose, we saw smoke coming from the beach, and a voice shouted out to us, "Hey there, did you catch anything for breakfast?"

We had no idea who the voice belonged to, but when we told him we had no fish, he recommended that we cast our net to the right side of the boat. It seemed a bit strange, but we didn't have anything to lose, so we did just as he said. Sure enough, we caught more fish than we could haul in.

It was then that my friend John suddenly realized who it was we were speaking to. "It's the Lord!" he yelled.

I had to be first to get to Jesus, so, without stopping to think, I threw on my clothes, jumped in the lake, and swam to shore.[1]

And there he was—Jesus on the beach, with a smile on his face, cooking up a storm over a charcoal fire. It took me back to that painful evening when I stood warming myself by a charcoal fire in the court-yard—just before Jesus was crucified.[2] Just before I messed up.

I took a moment to warm myself beside the fire, while my friends brought in the boat with a net full of fish. Realizing they might need a hand, I ran over and dragged the heavy net ashore, as Jesus called out to us, "Come join me—breakfast is ready!"[3]

This is one of the most intimate scenes in all of Scripture—a picture of true friendship, as those who deserted Jesus are now invited again into deep fellowship. It's also a story of deep change—the kind of change required if we are to imitate Jesus, become spiritual leaders, and bring others into shared spiritual leadership with us.

In the previous chapter, we concluded with a summary of the three generative principles practiced by adaptive spiritual leaders. The first of these is *becoming spiritual leaders through experiencing and modeling deep change.* Over the next few pages, we will explore how Peter illustrates this principle and consider together some key practices that can help us live it out.

PETER'S TRANSFORMATION

Because of his prominence in Scripture, it is easy for us to put someone like Peter on a pedestal. But Peter was not always the leader we eventually see him become. Peter went from being a brash, self-absorbed fisherman to a humble, compassionate, and courageous leader. It's clear from the Gospel accounts that Peter already had leadership potential. At times, he got things really right—it was Simon Peter who declared Jesus as the Messiah, Son of the Living God. In that moment Jesus gave him a new name—"the rock"— and with it, a new identity.

In the following scene, however, Jesus tells Peter to, "Get behind me, Satan!" Peter is rebuked for suggesting that Jesus shouldn't go to Jerusalem to suffer and die. Jesus goes on to call Peter a "stumbling block"—because he has only human rather than divine concerns in mind.[4] How can the same guy go from being "the rock" in one scene to being likened to Satan in the next? If we're honest with ourselves, is not this dualistic, conflicted, hypocritical version of leadership familiar to many of us in our own lives and expressions of leadership?

But Peter undergoes significant transformation, as evidenced by his exhortations to others late in his life. In his first letter to them, Peter urges the believers scattered across Asia Minor to be holy, just as God is holy, and reminds them they have been born anew, imperishable, through the living and enduring word of God.[5] Peter declares their new identity as a chosen race, a royal priesthood, a holy nation, as God's own people that they may proclaim God's mighty acts in the world. He reminds them of Jesus' suffering and encourages them as they suffer to not be fearful or intimidated, but to set apart Christ as Lord, always being ready to give an account of their hope with gentleness and respect.[6] Then, he tells them to continue to love and serve one another with the strength that God supplies.[7] He concludes by exhorting the elders to tend the flock of God, not by lording it over, but in humility and by being an example, reminding them of the way of Jesus, the chief Shepherd.[8]

This encouragement comes from a leader who finally reached the end of himself and experienced deep change. It comes from a follower of Jesus who decided his life was no longer his own. It comes from a man who was passionately in love with the One who loved him.

TRANSFORMED TO TRANSFORM

Experiencing deep personal change is vital because it's only when we have experienced that transformation ourselves that we can give it away. All of us want to see positive change in the lives of others and the systems and organizations we live within and lead, but *we must be transformed ourselves if we want to be transforming.* As we consider this principle, we will revisit and integrate many of the ideas from previous chapters.

This transformation centers around learning to love, lead, and follow like Jesus.

LOVE: THE WAY OF JESUS

Think again of that moment on the beach, with Jesus cooking breakfast for his disciples. Perhaps Peter is still wet from his impetuous swim to shore. Perhaps the disciples are telling stories and laughing with Jesus as they eat. After breakfast, Jesus turns to Peter and asks, "'Simon son of John, do you love me more than these?'" (John 21:15a). With the same smell of charcoal in the air as that night he denied Jesus, and beside the same lake where Jesus originally called him, imagine what Peter was thinking and feeling.

RESTORED TO RELATIONSHIP

Do you love me? It's an interesting question, under the circumstances. Perhaps most of us would be more inclined to ask, *Are you sorry?* or *Why did you fail me?* or *What were you thinking?* These questions would likely have prompted shame, but it is clear this was not Jesus' intention. It is God's *kindness* (not his judgment) that leads us to repentance.[9] Jesus' primary concern seems to be restoring relationship. Earlier in this book we considered Paul's appeal in Philippians 2: *Have you any encouragement from being united with Christ? Have you any comfort from his love? Have you any fellowship with his Spirit?* Paul is encapsulating precisely what Jesus is doing with Peter in this scene— elevating relationship, and particularly love, above anything else.

Jesus asks Peter three questions, and the text says that, by the third, Peter is grieved.[10] There is an obvious correlation between Jesus' three questions about Peter's love and Peter's three denials prior to the Crucifixion. Jesus is clearly inviting Peter to *restored relationship.* It's likely that Peter entered this conversation thinking he was disqualified from being part of what Jesus is doing in the world— he's fishing again, at the same lake! Given his failure, it seems he is resigned to the fact that he must return to his old life. While *Jesus* is not shaming Peter, my guess is that *Peter* has been heaping shame upon himself since that dreadful day when he denied his Lord. Jesus is actually inviting Peter back to himself in love.

WHAT KIND OF LOVE?

Although Jesus asks three similar questions, they are not identical. In English, we only have one word for *love.* However, in Greek, which is the language of the New Testament, there are several words for *love.* We discussed one of these in chapter three as the key characteristic of the unity found in the Trinity. That same word is used by all of the New Testament writers to indicate the kind of love we are called to embody. This is *agape* love.[11] In the first instance in this scene, Jesus asks Peter, "Do you *agape* me?" Peter responds, however, "Yes Lord; you know that I *philéō* you." *Philéō* is the root of the word *Philadelphia*, which is the city of brotherly love. Rather than a divine kind of love (*agape),* Peter affirms a brotherly love or the love between friends. A second time, Jesus asks, "Do you *agape* me?" Peter responds, "Yes Lord; you know that I *philéō* you." The third time, though, Jesus asks, "Do you *philéō* me." Peter, grieved by this revised question, responds, "Lord you know everything; you know that I *philéō* you."[12]

When we appreciate the subtleties in the text, it reads quite differently. I hear it like this:

> *Peter, do you love me in a God-like way, like I love you?*
> Lord, you know that I love you like a friend, like a brother.
> *Peter, do you love me in a God-like way, like I love you?*
> Lord, you know that I love you like a friend, like a brother.
> *Peter, do you love me like a friend and a brother?*
> Lord, you know that I do. I just jumped in the lake and swam to shore—
> I certainly love you, Lord. I just don't love you the way you love me.

Peter doesn't see divine love in himself, so Jesus meets him where he is. Jesus is Immanuel, God with us, and comes to where Peter is rather than asking Peter to come to him. In doing so, however, Jesus is inviting Peter to something deeper. He is inviting Peter to divine love, to perfect love.

WHAT'S IN A NAME?

There's another interesting detail in the text that is easy to miss. Notice how Jesus addresses Peter each time he asks him these questions: "Simon son of John."[13] As far as we know, Jesus has not referred to Peter this way since Jesus changed his name in John 1:42—when Jesus first called the disciples to follow him. On the day of that initial calling, they were standing at the Sea of Galilee (Tiberias) where Peter fished,[14] and now Jesus and Peter stand along the same shore. Peter was there to fish—not as a diversion, but as an occupation. If Peter was considering a return to his former life, how do you imagine he felt when Jesus called him Simon son of John?

I think this would have gotten Peter's attention. Without having to actually say it, Jesus seems to be asking which one of these people Peter wants to be. *Do you want to embrace the identity and nature I've given you, or do you want to go back?*

Do you ever find yourself back on that shore? Wondering whether you are now disqualified? Feeling nothing but shame? Remember, Jesus wasn't shaming Peter; he was restoring Peter to his true identity, nature, and calling.

But Peter had a choice, just as we do. This is a critical decision point for a spiritual leader. This is a *deep change* moment.

Let me detour from Peter's story and tell you another bit of mine. I've already mentioned that I grew up with tremendous insecurities. Perhaps like Peter, I could not see what Jesus sees in me. (This seems to be true for many of us.) It was not hard for me to believe that God loves other people … but me? In the midst of my insecurities, when I looked in the mirror I saw "never enough" rather than "loved by God." I craved the approval of others and seldom lived up to my own expectations—or the perceived expectations of others.

In my early twenties, I had an encounter with the Lord that was almost like a second conversion for me. It was most certainly a fresh work of grace. I was employed in a church as a worship leader, yet I felt a million miles from the Lord. I was trying to be authentic, but I felt like an imposter. Every week I would stand in front of the congregation and wonder whether people could see through the mask I was wearing. One day, while desperately seeking the Lord, I felt led to 2 Corinthians where Paul says, "God made him who had no sin to be sin for us, so that in him we might become the righteousness of God" (2 Corinthians 5:21 NIV). Although I'd been raised in church, somehow I had always assumed that righteousness was something I had to attain. But in that moment, it was as if the words jumped off the page to me. Righteousness is not something I attain but something God gives if we are "in him"—that is, "in Christ." This is our identity! We are the righteousness of God in Christ.

My friends Ron and Bonnie Crandall like to describe this identity in this way: You are a COGPOW! *A child of God and a person of worth.* This special couple believe that if people can truly understand and see themselves as made in the image of God and loved by God, it changes everything. It changes not only the way we see ourselves, but also the way we see everyone we meet. We may assume others are made in the image of God, but do we treat them that way? If I am a COGPOW, then so are you. So are my children. So are my students. So are my neighbors. So, even, are my enemies.

Jesus' own identity was secure. At his baptism, the Spirit descended upon Jesus like a dove, and the Father spoke these words over him: "This is my Son, whom I love; with him I am well pleased" (Matthew 3:17 NIV). Jesus had done *no* public ministry at this time. The Father's pleasure had nothing to do with what Jesus had or had not done; it was purely based on his love for his Son. Jesus was a COGPOW!

In Peter's encounter with the resurrected Jesus on the shore, it seems Jesus is trying to help Peter see himself as he is: Jesus' beloved. Before his death, Jesus had invited Peter and the other disciples to abide in his love in the same way Jesus abides in the Father's love.[15] This is the beginning point of the Cycle of Love we examined in chapter four. Before we can do anything else, including love ourselves or love others, we must *encounter* the love of God, the very God of love. If we are ever to lead others as a means of grace and create an environment for shared spiritual leadership, we must first *encounter* this love in grace.

What prevents us from encountering God in this way and truly seeing ourselves the way God sees us? Many of us have received messages from our family of origin or have had experiences in life that prompt these "never enough" scripts. We may have a proclivity toward such scripts in our per-sonalities. Whatever the cause, these scripts are obstacles that block us from encountering and sharing the love of God.

Peter needed this fresh *encounter* with Jesus that day on the shore not only to restore his identity in Christ but also to help him become all that Jesus was calling him to be. Peter was being invited to deep change by an experience of deep love.

LEAD: SHEPHERD LIKE JESUS

As Peter responded to each of the three questions about love, Jesus invited him to "shepherd." The call from Jesus was to "feed my lambs," "tend my sheep," and "feed my sheep."[16] Notice the invitation to both care for and pro-tect the sheep inherent in these statements. Peter was not a shepherd. In fact, this is quite a different metaphor from Jesus' original invitation to Peter (and the other disciples) to "fish for people."[17] The fishing metaphor had its own implications and certainly fit the context that Peter knew well. Jesus was speaking Peter's language. In this scene, however, Jesus is now calling Peter to something outside his comfort zone.

While Peter had never been a shepherd, he had certainly been watching the Good Shepherd.

The language of shepherding as leadership is used throughout Scripture.[18] Jesus is the Good Shepherd who lays down his life for his sheep.[19] He sacrifices in a selfless, loving way for the sake of others. This is the demonstration of kenosis we have already discussed.[20]

Jesus is calling Peter to relational leadership based in selfless love. This invitation, by its very nature, is empowering. Jesus is reminding Peter, who is likely feeling disqualified and ashamed, that he is still called to tend and feed Jesus' sheep. In his lifetime, Jesus chose to deeply impact just a few lives in a relatively small geographical area. However, he trusted that, by the Spirit, these misfit followers would be able to change the world. Jesus created and maintained an environment that fostered relationship, growth, formation, development, empowerment, and experimentation for his disciples. That is that kind of leading/shepherding that he is inviting Peter into in these moments.

FOLLOW: BEING DISCIPLES FIRST

In John 21, Jesus is inviting Peter not only to lead, but also to *follow*. Jesus hints at the way in which Peter will die, and then he simply says to him, "Follow me."[21] As was common for Peter, he objects, and asks Jesus about John's fate.[22] Jesus says, "If it is my will that he remain until I come, what is that to you? Follow me!" (John 21:22). These are the same words Jesus used to call Peter in the first place,[23] yet they seem to have a different implication now. That first invitation to "follow me" required a great deal of the disciples, but it was an invitation to "come and see."[24] This post-resurrection invitation to follow Jesus, as Dietrich Bonhoeffer explains, is a call to "come and die."[25] For Peter, this would not be a figurative death. Jesus had already demonstrated his willingness to die on the cross, and now he points to a similar fate for Peter.

Jesus is summoning Peter to follow him in a way that will cost him everything. It will require a deeper kind of love; a selfless, life-giving (*agape*) love that is more than a mere human kind of love. As Jesus said, "No one has greater love than this, to lay down one's life for one's friends" (John 15:13). Jesus not only demonstrated this *agape* love, but he is also inviting Peter to it. The picture of deep change is getting clearer.

At the beginning of the chapter, I mentioned that I had the opportunity to serve as a missionary in India. I had a strong sense of call to go, but no confidence that I would ever return. In fact, while we didn't discuss it together until later, my wife shared the same fear. Would I die traveling? Would I lose my life while sharing my faith? I didn't know. Many of us grew up with a theology that says that God will always protect us if we are doing God's will; but that didn't work out so well for many of Jesus' followers. For instance, despite being Jesus' cousin, John the Baptist lost his head while in the middle of God's will.[26] As I thought about responding to God's call, all of these fears came to mind. Was I willing to die for the gospel? As a worship leader, I routinely urged people to give themselves as a living sacrifice in response to God's love and mercy,[27] but, when push came to shove, was I really willing to give everything? I experienced a crisis of faith—a deep-change moment. I had to decide whether following Jesus was truly my most important and fundamental priority or just one among many.

One key to *following* is acknowledging that *spiritual leaders are authentic disciples first.* No one ever graduates from being a disciple of Jesus; we don't one day cease to be disciples and become leaders. *Following* well requires us to let go of control and let Jesus be Lord. It requires us to continually be learning and growing.

Because this order is critical, we will focus on *following before leading* for the remainder of this chapter.

INTEGRATING LOVING, FOLLOWING, AND LEADING

It could almost appear as if Jesus is making three different points in John 21: loving, following, and leading. But these three dynamics are interconnected—as modeled by Jesus himself.

Loving. The Gospel of John tells us how Jesus knows he is loved: he abides in the Father's love. He returns that love to the Father but also gives it away to others. The context of the relationship between the Father and the Son is holy love. Jesus lives within this relationship not just some of the time, but *all* of the time. He doesn't merely come into the Father's presence to get refreshed and refueled; he abides in the Father's presence constantly. He lives this love with his disciples constantly as well. They abide in Jesus' love in the same way that Jesus abides in the Father's love. This is the core of their relationship.[28] Jesus answers the question, "Do you love *(agape)* me?" by saying *yes* to the Father. This is Jesus' invitation to Peter and to us too.

Following. We all see Jesus as a leader, but he is a follower first. In John 5, explaining to his disciples that he can only do what he sees the Father doing, he says, "I can do nothing on my own."[29] As with the three-year-old I mentioned earlier, Jesus was simply imitating his Daddy. What if we saw ourselves in that way? What if we were that dependent upon God as true followers? What if I understood that I have no capacity to lead others unless I *do what I see* the Father doing and *speak what I hear* the Father speaking? This is the kind of leader Jesus was. Jesus was essentially saying to Peter—as he says to us now—"Follow me in the same way I follow the Father."

Leading. Jesus demonstrated leading for his disciples. Like a shepherd, he protects and cares for his sheep. He knows them by name, and they know him—even by his voice. He lays down his life for them. The environment Jesus created allowed his disciples to be in true relationship with him. He is showing them how to lead *through* challenges and has invited his team to lead with him in facing those challenges. As the Good Shepherd, Jesus demonstrates leadership based not on control but on empowerment.[30] It is into this kind of leadership that Jesus invites Peter—and invites us as well.

Jesus modeled this integration of loving, following, and leading, and he restores Peter's identity and calling so that Peter can embody this integration himself. In the process, Peter experiences deep change. He is forever transformed. Only when this transformation occurs can Peter model it for others. The same is true for each of us.

HELPFUL PRACTICES

How can we practically experience deep change and grow our spiritual leadership? How do we say yes to the invitation of Jesus to love, follow, and lead … and what does it require of us?

Early in this book we looked at Philippians 2 and Paul's invitation to *empty* ourselves (kenosis) as Jesus did. This is a great place to start. Embodying this kind of kenotic leadership is precisely what Jesus was inviting Peter to in their interaction by the lake, and it's what Peter and the other early church leaders did in Acts 6 and Acts 15 as they practiced shared spiritual leadership amid their challenges. Shared spiritual leadership requires the integration of loving, following, and leading together. Three intentional practices come to mind for me that enable us to become spiritual leaders: *abiding, humility,* and *courage.*

Abiding. Jesus said, "Abide in me, as I abide in you … Those who abide in me and I in them bear much fruit, because apart from me you can do nothing" (John 15:4–5). We've been discussing what it means to abide throughout this book, and I encourage you to consider how you are doing this as a spiritual leader. Are you abiding in Jesus as he abides in you, and abiding in Jesus' love just as he abides in the Father's love? Like Peter, do you need restoration in your identity in Christ—or in your calling? Are you experiencing "union with Christ"? Is your identity secure as a Child of God and Person of Worth (COGPOW)? Remember: We must *encounter* the love of God before we can give it away.

As an authentic follower of Jesus, are you practicing the means of grace? Do you have a pattern, place, and people that help you live in union with Christ? Are you passionately pursuing Jesus as a disciple first?

Humility. As we abide in Christ, we are invited to practice *humility.* In previous chapters we have not only discussed the idea of kenosis, but we have looked at the ways Jesus and his followers lived out kenosis in the book of Acts. How, practically, can we embody kenosis?

Philippians 2:6–11 is sometimes called the Kenosis Hymn.[31] In it we see this pattern:

- the privileged status of Jesus;
- Jesus' self-emptying; and
- God exalting Jesus.

These verses make it clear that Jesus existed "in the form of God," while having "equality with God," yet he did not regard that equality as something to "be exploited."[32] It seems to me there are at least two key things to ponder here. First, practicing humility is surrendering privilege and status. Second, humility is serving others in love. Are you living in humility and embodying sacrificial love with others? Are you maturing toward divine love? Are you emptying yourself for the sake of others? What are you being asked to surrender in response to God's love? Practically, are there privileges that you can lay down rather than exploit?

The Kenosis Hymn also makes it clear that Jesus took the "form" of a servant. The same word is used to indicate that Jesus existed in the "form" of God. This is not impersonation. Jesus didn't merely act like one who served; he actually took on the very nature of a servant. In response to God's love, are you truly a servant in the way you live and lead, or do you merely act like a servant some of the time?

Another aspect of Jesus' humility we are called to imitate is empowerment. Rather than hoarding power for himself, love moved Jesus to empower those he led. He promised them the same empowerment from the Holy Spirit that he experienced. Paul and Peter both noticed this and gave authority and responsibility to those they led. Imitating Jesus, they led with both humility and confidence. So, are you empowered by the Spirit and empowering to others? Do you lead relationally in love with both humility and confidence?

The Kenosis Hymn concludes with exaltation. As a result of Jesus' emptying of himself, his humility, and his death on the cross, God exalted him to the highest place and gave him the highest name. This is a biblical principle that shows up throughout the New Testament: those who humble themselves will be exalted.[33] Jesus, though, is the Christ and has the name above all names; at the name of Jesus, every knee shall bow and tongue confess that he is Lord![34] Notice that it is God who does the exalting or lifting up. We do not need to do this ourselves. As we practice humility, the Lord will provide opportunities for us to shine as his servants.

Courage. As we practice abiding and humility, the Lord fills and empowers us to love, follow, and lead with boldness and courage. Remember again that the consistent theme in the book of Acts is that as the early church disciples were filled with the Spirit, they became bold witnesses.[35] The ability to be courageous is a byproduct of the Spirit's activity in our lives, and it often increases as we share a missional purpose with others.

People generally assume that courage is the opposite of fear. In the Scripture, though, it is *perfect love* that overcomes fear.[36] We practice courage as it is given to us through the love of God. Erwin McManus contends that courage is not the absence of fear but instead the absence of self.[37] You see, courage comes as we are filled with the love of God and love of others, and realize that our calling and purpose to serve in love is more important than our own lives.

Let's look at Peter again. As he continued to follow Jesus, Peter discovered what Edwin Friedman calls *differentiated leadership.*[38] Peter grew confident in his own identity and calling and was able to maintain a "non-anxious presence" in the midst of highly anxious situations. He led with courage and confidence, yet he remained humble. He was not pulled into the anxiety of others or overwhelmed by fear but he remained meaningfully and lovingly connected with others.[39] Like Jesus, Peter and the early church leaders who practiced shared leadership with him persevered through their greatest adaptive challenges with courage in the love of God.

Practically speaking, all of us have fears. The reason the early church needed boldness and courage is because they kept becoming afraid. This is human nature. As we abide and surrender, only then can the Holy Spirit fill and empower us to boldness and courage. Do you exhibit courage and perseverance in the face of challenge? Rather than mustering your own courage, how can you let go of control and trust God to lead and love through you? What keeps you from loving and leading courageously? Is it insecurity? Is it a lack of trust? Is it fear of failure? Is it fear of success? Is it that you feel you are fighting alone? Truly following Jesus regularly leads us out of what is comfortable (status quo) and into the unknown. The real question is, do we trust God to lead and love through us? We do not do the work of the kingdom of God on our own. We only do so *with* God.

When we trust that only through God can we love, follow, and lead, then we can surrender our own agenda and control and begin to truly empower others courageously. We do so based on our shared relationship with Jesus as we abide, surrender, and serve others courageously in love.

I have intentionally posed a number of questions to reflect on in the past few pages. They are summarized in the graphic below.

LOVING

- Do you need restoration in your identity and calling?
- Are you experiencing "union with Christ"?
- Is your identity secure as a COGPOW (child of God — person of worth)?
- Are you living in humility and embodying love with others?
- Are you maturing toward divine love?

FOLLOWING

- Do you have a pattern, place, and people that help you live in union with Christ?
- Are you passionately pursuing Jesus as a disciple first?
- Are you emptying yourself for the sake of others?
- What are you being asked to surrender in response to God's love?
- Are there privileges that you can lay down rather than exploit?

LEADING

- Are you truly a servant in the way you lead or merely acting like a servant?
- Are you empowered by the Spirit and empowering to others?
- Do you lead relationally in love with both humility and confidence?
- Do you exhibit courage and perseverance in the face of challenge?
- Are you letting go of control?

Formational Accountability. Accountability is critical for leading together well. You may have noticed that the word "accountability" has already shown up several times throughout this book. This is because being held accountable is critical; and holding other people accountable, though one of the most important skills for leaders, is unfortunately absent in too many environments. Creating an environment for healthy and fruitful leading together requires three different types of accountability that increase our adaptive capacity: formational, relational, and missional. These three types of accountability coincide with our three generative principles: spiritual leaders, creating environments, and fruitful processes.

The key accountability in growing us as spiritual leaders is *formational accountability*, which is intentional accountability around our spiritual formation and growth.[40] As SLI have facilitated change in many different churches and organizations, instituting a system of formational accountability is consistently named as the most transformative element of the process. It is primarily through formational accountability that we are vulnerable with one another about our lives and are continually transformed by the Spirit's work. Although there are a number of ways to facilitate accountability for spiritual growth, some keys to remember are the importance of asking deep questions, identifying specific areas where accountability is needed, and checking back in on those areas regularly. Our questions can focus on how we are abiding in Jesus, how we are practicing humility, and how we are embodying love with others courageously. Accountability moves us from merely a desire to love, follow, and lead like Jesus to actually putting it into practice with others.

KENOSIS AS IMITATION

Think back now on our music metaphor. Jesus was the master jazz musician, and Peter and Paul were both mimicking the master. At the same time, they were willing for people to mimic them. In fact, they both encouraged others to follow their example. Without someone to imitate, many of us will never know what it can practically look like to love, follow, and lead like Jesus.

A critical component of spiritual leadership is *modeling a life for others to imitate*. However, this must be a byproduct of our loving and following personally and not merely an attempt to show off. Paul often asserts his authority as an apostle as he begins his letters,[41] but his opening greeting to the Philippian church makes his agenda clear. He begins by saying, "Paul and Timothy, slaves of Christ Jesus ... " (Philippians 1:1a). We have already discussed Paul's challenge to this church to be like Jesus, who emptied himself and took the "form" of a slave. Paul introduced himself and his protégé as slaves as well. After the Kenosis Hymn in the same letter, he identifies Timothy as one who served in the work of the gospel[42] and Epaphroditus, one who had been sent to Paul from the church in Philippi, as one who "came close to death for the work of Christ" (Philippians 2:30).[43] Here Paul lifts up these two companions as ones who exhibited the same kind of self-emptying (kenosis) that we see in Jesus.

Paul seems to have known that the idea of being like Jesus as portrayed in the Kenosis Hymn would be overwhelming to most followers of Jesus. He could hear people wondering, *Can I really become like Jesus?* He wanted to demonstrate to them that, by the work of grace, this truly is possible. I can imagine him saying to those in the church in Philippi: *Before you dismiss this idea of being like Jesus, I want to show you some living examples. These are people you know. Remember Timothy and your own Epaphroditus. You know they have emptied themselves and slave away in love for the sake of the gospel. You have seen it. This can be true for you, too. Imitate them even as they imitate Jesus.*

In the chapter following the Kenosis Hymn, as he does in other letters, Paul invites his readers to look at his life.[44] He essentially provides his own résumé, claiming that if anyone has reason to boast in the flesh, he has more because of his own heritage, zeal, and righteousness under the law.[45] Paul demonstrates how he exchanged everything for the "surpassing value" of knowing Jesus and being identified with him.[46] He names the "prize of the heavenly call of God in Christ Jesus," which is precisely what Paul is moving toward, and he calls those in the church to do the same. He concludes this section with this challenge: "Brothers and sisters, join in imitating me, and observe those who live according to the example you have in us" (Philippians 3:17).

Inviting others to imitate us as leaders is difficult for many of us. It is also a delicate balance. For some this is a challenge because we do not want to appear arrogant. But when we look at Paul, we see that this invitation to imitation is clothed with great humility. For others of us, this is daunting because we're aware that we do not yet live and love like Jesus. The balance is found by inviting imitation while also admitting we're still on the journey of becoming like Jesus. This was Paul's approach and should be ours, too.

People are watching us—whether we are parents, mentors, older siblings, pastors, or leaders in other sectors, both formally and informally. Simply put, *we have influence in the lives of others.* As we think about this influence and our desire to model the right kind of behavior, we can be tempted to *fake* our way through. We can put on a mask and *act the part* of a leader for people to see, while we are living lives in private that do not represent Christ. Here is the key: *Model not for the sake of others, but simply to pursue Jesus.* This pursuit always bears the fruit of serving others in love. As we mimic Jesus the master, we will model a life for others to mimic. This happens most effectively in the context of shared leadership.

COMING FULL CIRCLE: BEARING FRUIT

We have looked at Jesus, Peter, Paul, Timothy, and Epaphroditus as examples of those who embody kenosis. This is possible for us too. But remember, this must begin with our being united with Christ in abiding. *Union precedes kenosis.* We must *encounter* the God of love. *Emptying* ourselves is a response to this encounter. We adopt the posture of humility because only Jesus saves and only the Holy Spirit brings transformation. We humble ourselves and take the "form" of a servant—not merely acting like one who serves. This *emptying* of self means laying down any of our own privilege, status, and power that can be exploited or used for our advantage.

In this emptied state, we *love, follow,* and *lead* with confidence, boldness, and courage, because we are secure in the love of God and the righteousness of Christ. We know our identity and calling. We live boldly as we have been filled and *empowered* by the Holy Spirit such that we *embody* the love of God with others.

Bearing this kind of fruit often comes through *works of mercy* that we discussed in chapter four, which are themselves a means of grace. These include attending to the least, the last, and the lost by means of feeding the hungry, clothing the naked, entertaining the stranger, and visiting those who are sick and in prison. We also embody this fruit of love in simple acts of kindness with our families, our team, our neighbors, and even our enemies.

Jesus invited Peter to tend and care for his sheep. Late in his life, Peter challenges those following him to become shepherds as well:

> I exhort the elders among you to tend the flock of God that is in your charge, exercising the oversight, not under compulsion but willingly, as God would have you do it—not for sordid gain but eagerly. Do not lord it over those in your charge but be examples to the flock.

1 Peter 5:1b–3

Peter then says, "the God of all grace, who has called you to his eternal glory in Christ, will himself restore, support, strengthen, and establish you" (1 Peter 5:10).

Peter had discovered the joy of emptying himself and had experienced the fruit of loving, following, and leading like Jesus with others. His life was no longer his own. Instead, he had been completely transformed by the God of love. In the opening verses of his second letter, Peter says, "His divine power has given us everything needed for life and godliness, through the knowledge of him who called us by his own glory and goodness" (2 Peter 1:3). He goes on to state that we are to become "participants of the divine nature" (2 Peter 1:4). We are participating in the very life of God, abiding in Jesus, in step with and bearing the fruit of the Spirit as spiritual leaders. In so doing, we are becoming more and more like Jesus, and God's divine power has given us everything we need for that to happen.

The God of perfect (*agape*) love invites us to abide in Jesus' love in the same way that Jesus abides in the Father's love. We, like Peter, are invited to lead in the way of Jesus in selfless love. As we love, follow, and lead in this way, we can create the environment for others to do the same.

7

IMPROV AND COLLABORATION: CREATING TRANSFORMING ENVIRONMENTS

In the late 1990s, I was leading worship at a student camp in Colorado with my band. Many people were praying fervently for the students to encounter the Lord. In the middle of one of our worship sets, as the music was building to a crescendo and the students were pouring their hearts out to the Lord in worship, I sent a cue to our drummer. But Kyle, an incredible musician, missed it entirely. I turned slightly, in the hope of making eye contact with him, only to realize that he was not sitting at his drums. Startled by this, I continued to play but turned a bit further and found him on his knees with his hands lifted high in worship. Kyle was improvising; and his actions set the tone for how the Lord was moving in the room—a tone that had less to do with the music and more to do with an atmosphere of complete surrender. We watched as the students followed his example.

One of the most important roles of a spiritual leader is *creating environments that foster transformation*. This transformation is the work of the Spirit in us, making us more like Jesus individually and collectively, such that the world around us is changed. This transformation occurs in an environment of shared leadership, as we value and embody complementary gifts and strengths.

WHY ENVIRONMENTS MATTER

Have you ever noticed that greater focus and fruitfulness comes in certain kinds of environments? All of us are familiar with Netflix, and many of us are their loyal customers. Clearly the company has been wildly successful. But behind their success is an intentional environment and culture. Rather than focusing on financial incentives, they emphasize building a dream team in pursuit of ambitious common goals; and they prioritize a culture built on freedom and responsibility. The Netflix Manifesto,[1] which has been viewed over twenty million times, places people over process. One senior software engineer described working at Netflix in this way, "The environment encourages you to be a better version of yourself, which is far from the case in many places and often the opposite of that."[2] Modern companies, like Netflix, have sometimes understood better than the church the importance of fostering positive environments.[3]

Think about this practically. Effective parents are purposeful about the kind of environments in which their kids are raised. Worship leaders take seriously the environment they create for people to engage with the Lord. Businesses allocate time and resources to team-building and creating their corporate culture. Conversely, think about how many organizations were negatively affected by COVID-19 because their environments were ill-prepared to face such challenges.

As we have previously discussed, when transformation happens, it is the work of the Spirit.[4] The Holy Spirit can clearly work in any environment, but the environments we create can cooperate with the Spirit—or do the opposite.

Alan Roxburgh frames this well when he says there is a "recognition that leadership in the local church is less and less about creating and managing programs and then trying to get people into them and more and more about creating the environments that foster interconnections and conversations among people."[5]

A transformative environment is one in which healthy relationships are formed, and in which generative possibilities are created. Within these healthy relationships, people continually grow in their character, competency, and capacity. This kind of environment fosters discernment and change that brings about fruitfulness as people are able to face complex challenges. The environment itself creates the conditions in which transformation is possible.

In their book *A Church Called Tov,* Scot McKnight and Laura Barringer highlight how Christians have seen and experienced abuses of power in what were some of the most respected churches in the US. Their premise is that while pastors and leaders play a primary role in forming church culture, toxicity in a church is more about the culture itself than one person, one leader, or one event. Toxic church cultures tend to form people in subtle yet unhealthy ways, and often warnings signs are missed or dismissed.[6] These toxic cultures can be created or exacerbated by the celebrity status of a leader (especially the solo-heroic leader we explored earlier)—yet the congregation is complicit in this toxicity. The authors state,

Celebrities don't form on their own. Behind every celebrity pastor is an adoring congregation that both loves and supports the celebrity atmosphere. The development of a celebrity culture also doesn't happen overnight. It begins when a pastor has a driving ambition for fame, but it can't take root unless the congregation supports that ambition. Unfortunately, many people want their pastor to be a spiritual hero or a celebrity at some level. They not only want it, but they also expect it and find themselves believing it about their pastor. Some pastors devour this attention and take it to the next level.[7]

The warning signs of narcissism and power-mongering are often ignored as church leaders create false narratives to protect themselves, discredit their critics, and maintain their "brand." In contrast to this toxicity, McKnight and Barringer advocate for intentionally creating a "goodness culture" that is committed to cultivating empathy, grace, people above institution, truth, justice, service, and Christlikeness.

The abuses we see across the US church landscape illuminate the critical importance of creating a healthy environment and culture. Creating transforming environments allows leaders to invite others who share an adaptive challenge into a space where they can grow in relationship and trust in God and one another, and discern together what seems good to the Holy Spirit and to them. In such an environment, people have the courage to take the risks (steps of faith) that the Spirit leads them into together in union with Christ. As spiritual leaders embody kenosis in this environment, their clarity of identity, calling, and self-sacrificial love enables them to train up those who can train others,[8] which over time will have a generative effect in their context. So, an environment of Jesus-centered, shared spiritual leadership creates a healthy culture over time and allows leaders to not only face and overcome adaptive challenges but also to invest themselves in the next generation of spiritual leaders.

From a biblical perspective, consider the environment Jesus created with his disciples and why it was important. As we have discussed, it was an environment of deep trust and camaraderie that led to real friendships. Within those relationships, there was risk, adventure, challenge, mission, and fruitfulness. Jesus knew the power of the environment he created—both in fostering deep relationships and in equipping and preparing his disciples for the challenging mission ahead of them.[9]

So, are we creating environments that foster or inhibit growth and transformation? Are we intentionally creating healthy cultures, or do our churches/organizations exhibit the warning signs of a toxic culture? By creating environments that foster growth and transformation, we create the conditions in which the Trinity works in and through people's lives.

ENVIRONMENTS THAT TRANSFORM

Imagine getting a doctor's diagnosis that calls for radical changes in your lifestyle. Or having a vision for something that means you have to change your priorities and potentially your vocation. This tension is often fraught with both *pain* and *possibility*.

As we discussed in chapter five, adaptive tension disrupts equilibrium and status quo within a person, a family, a team, or an organization. It is within this disequilibrium—where we enter into the *liminal space* between where we've been and where we are called to be—that spiritual leaders can create the environment for adaptive leadership to thrive. Within this space, the Spirit works, adaptive capacity grows, and our greatest transformation is possible.

The early church leaders capitalized on the tension caused by their persecution and created environments that enabled new movement in the church in Antioch. Barnabas was sent to Antioch to exhort the believers to remain faithful and devoted to Jesus. He later returned with Saul (who became the apostle Paul), and they ministered there together.[10] Paul and Barnabas eventually went again to Antioch where they strengthened the disciples and reminded them, "It is through many persecutions that we must enter the kingdom of God" (Acts 14:22b). By empowering indigenous leaders in the church in Antioch, Paul and Barnabas also created an environment for shared leadership.[11]

The remainder of the book of Acts chronicles the continual challenges experienced in the ministries of Paul, Barnabas, Silas, Timothy, Luke, Lydia, Aquila, and Priscilla. Amid those challenges, we see environments created for hospitality,[12] for correction with grace,[13] for the gospel going to new places,[14] and for counter-cultural and sacrificial witness. Paul and Silas exemplified this when, imprisoned for their faith, they prayed and sang hymns while the other prisoners listened. Imagine how Paul and Silas shaped the prison environment! At around midnight the power of God shook the prison and set them free; but rather than escaping, Paul and Silas stayed and led the jailer and his entire household to faith.[15]

This is the power of creating transforming environments; it leads to the transformation of lives, of families, of organizations, and the world. In Acts 17:6, those in the early church were described as "turning the world upside down" (ESV), and this is precisely what the world needs again now.

WHAT'S IN THE ATMOSPHERE?

Management scholar Frank Barrett points out that a jazz band is a prototype for collaboration and improvisation. Playing jazz requires

trust and shared values, and is characterized by a dynamic tension between chaos and order (chaordic). It requires a commitment to discovering better alternatives, so musicians must be agile and adaptive. This
is the nature of improvisation, which requires living on the edge of the
unknown. A great jazz band can embrace chaos because of their deep trust
in their fellow musicians; in such an environment, they can improvise well
together.[16]

Heifetz and Linsky describe this sort of atmosphere as a "holding environment," within which the heat of tension or conflict can be adjusted: "A
holding environment is a space formed by a network of relationships within
which people can tackle tough, sometimes divisive questions without flying
apart."[17] Living within the disequilibrium of adaptive tension requires such
a holding environment.

In a work environment there can be sharp disagreement about which
strategy to use in a particular scenario. In the natural course of events, without a healthy holding environment, this disagreement could lead to mistrust
and ineffectiveness. However, if a healthy atmosphere is created, where individuals listen to conflicting perspectives and align around shared values, it is
possible that the tension itself can lead to better solutions and greater trust
in relationships.

In a church context, a holding environment is a space that is safe enough
for real conversation about adaptive challenges. In too many churches, unhealthy environments lead to extreme reactions. Either people are afraid to
discuss difficult challenges because of how it could negatively affect relationships; or, if difficult conversations do occur, they are often unhealthy and po-
larizing. Both of these extremes illustrate the need for a healthy atmosphere,
where there is enough trust for crucial conversations to occur, and a set of
guidelines to facilitate such conversations.

Creating a holding environment requires both *internal* and *external* fac-
tors to be addressed by those in a position of leadership. As Heifetz and his
colleagues write in *The Practice of Adaptive Leadership,* "You need to be able
to: (1) manage yourself in that environment and (2) help people tolerate
the discomfort they are experiencing."[18]

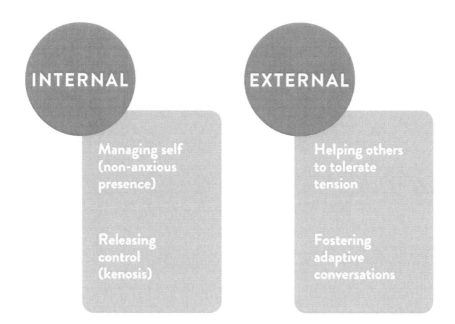

INTERNAL

Managing self
(non-anxious
presence)

Releasing
control
(kenosis)

EXTERNAL

Helping others
to tolerate
tension

Fostering
adaptive
conversations

Internally, healthy leaders will create a holding environment by managing self, and therefore maintaining a non-anxious presence amid the tension. As Bolsinger reminds us, experiencing sabotage and resistance is normal when leading adaptive change, and we must remember not to take this personally.[19] A spiritual leader must be able to step back from the tension and view the resistance more systemically. This keeps us from getting defensive, as well as keeping us from getting pulled into others' dysfunctions. If we are successful, we are able to maintain our own identity as a self-differentiated leader, while also remaining meaningfully connected with those we lead.[20]

In a particularly difficult season in my own leadership journey, I experienced sabotage and was tempted to become defensive and to take everything personally. In this context, functioning with a non-anxious presence as a self-differentiated leader was only possible because of the healthy holding environment of team.

A spiritual leader facing adaptive challenges must learn to release control. As we discussed earlier in this book, this is particularly challenging for the solo-heroic leader. Releasing control requires the kind of humility (kenosis) that we see in leaders who both trust the Lord and trust others. It also requires the patience and perseverance to stick with the process of adaptive leadership until solutions emerge.

Externally, leaders will help create a holding environment by supporting others who are having trouble tolerating the discomfort of adaptive tension. This is both a pastoral role that demonstrates the empathy of shared experience and also a prophetic role that asks tough questions and helps a team clearly name adaptive challenges. It requires the abiding, humility, and courage we discussed in the previous chapter. Notice the focus on the people and caring for their souls, while not neglecting the real challenges that must be faced if the team's mission is to be accomplished. This requires a recognition that people often experience loss during a season of adaptive change, and we must be present with them amid that loss. It also requires a resolve to press through the challenges together to discern new possibilities.

Supporting others while fostering adaptive conversations allows for productivity amid tension. Heifetz refers to this as *the productive zone of disequilibrium*.[21] The key is to keep the temperature high enough to reach a threshold of change without allowing the tension to boil over.[22] We want to make sure that we don't give in to the temptation to treat the adaptive challenge as a technical problem. This can happen early in an adaptive process or can creep into the response through "work avoidance"—where we either ignore the real challenge or keep ourselves busy with technical work instead of sticking with the issue long enough to find a solution. The zone of productivity is typically quite narrow for a team that is not used to doing adaptive work. The leader must therefore watch for the moments when the tension exceeds the limit of tolerance and lower the temperature when it does. Practically, this may mean pulling back from a conversation that begins to boil over and scheduling a follow-up conversation at a later time.

Just as an athlete strengthens a set of muscles through use, a team that has a strong holding environment will, over time, increase its adaptive capacity. They will be able to tolerate more and more tension without boiling over and will be able to stick with the adaptive tension for longer periods of time. In a local church, a team with a strong holding environment will care for one another in difficult times but also stay focused on overcoming the challenges they face in their mission.

COMMUNITAS AS A TRANSFORMATIVE ENVIRONMENT

The kind of environment we want to create incorporates deep trust, shared humility, dynamic learning, and courageous risk-taking. If we are in the right environment when facing adaptive challenges, we grow in *interdependence*. Alan Hirsch indicates that the early church created such an environment as they faced their own liminality and the dangers of persecution. Referencing the work of Victor Turner, Hirsch describes the resulting environment as *communitas*. This goes beyond a mere sense of community and occurs when a group formed around a shared purpose faces a shared ordeal (such as walking through an adaptive challenge).[23]

In the Euro 2020 Championship during the summer of 2021, Danish midfielder Christian Erikson collapsed on the pitch in the forty-third minute of the game against Finland. After suffering a cardiac arrest, Erikson was resuscitated. For his teammates, an important game suddenly became insignificant, as they worried about their friend. Thankfully, at the time of writing, Erikson is recovering; but the ordeal created a deep atmosphere of camaraderie and even greater friendship among members of the team.[24] While the team lost that particular game, their tournament success exceeded expectations.

We see this kind of environment of *communitas* throughout the book of Acts: people are known to one another, they share everything in common, they boldly risk their own lives for the sake of mission, and they have constant stories to tell of their own transformation. They also come to realize that, together, they are smarter and more effective at facing challenges and fulfilling mission than they could have ever been apart. They experience the unity that mirrors the very life of the Trinity.

HELPFUL PRACTICES

Integrating knowledge into action is often described as wisdom. Woodward and White say, "Leading through any kind of change takes wisdom .... Part of what it means to be a leader is to cultivate an environment where change is normal .... Managing change requires prayer, preparation and planning."[25]

As a reminder from the iceberg image, fruitfulness is the *outcome* we desire, while the *principles* are the fundamental convictions and beliefs we hold. If we are to see fruitfulness, we must put those principles into action through intentional *practices* that are guided and empowered by the Spirit. Let's look at some key practices you might implement in order to create transforming environments.

BUILDING HEALTHY TEAM

When you enter into a worship space, can you tell if it is healthy? As you begin a new small group experience, are you able to sense whether it is a safe place to belong? Many of us intuitively know whether or not an environment is healthy.

Building a healthy team is a critical practice for creating environments that foster transformation.[26] There is a clear assumption throughout this chapter and even this book that a team is necessary to overcome adaptive challenges and more effectively and fruitfully fulfill the purpose to which God has called us. Before recruiting a team, clarifying the "why" or purpose of the team is critical, because it is passion for a shared purpose that most prompts commitment. Without a clear purpose, teams may enjoy one another, but they cannot experience the *communitas* that only comes through traversing challenges within a shared purpose. Remember: team is where both growth and relationship (love) come together with shared responsibility in mission (purpose).

A side note here may be helpful. Perhaps you desire to build a healthy team that can lead together through adaptive challenges, but feel you are stuck with whatever committee or board is already in place. Here is a suggestion: Consider letting your existing board continue their work[27] but cast a vision for an additional team to work specifically on solutions to your adaptive challenges.

Assuming you have free reign to build a team, here are a few key steps to take to assure health:

- Pray. Jesus spent the night in prayer prior to recruiting members of his team.[28] You need the wisdom that comes through prayer, too.
- Be clear on the team's purpose.
- Recruit people who share a passion for the team's purpose, which can lead to high commitment and unity.
- Seek diversity to increase impact and effectiveness. Look for people with complementary gifts, perspectives, and skills around that shared passion and purpose.[29] (See Appendix A on Building Healthy Teams for a more detailed look at a process that accompanies these bullet points.)

Considering all of this, is the purpose of your team clear? How has prayer informed your team recruiting? Is each person on your team passionate about your shared purpose? Within that unity of shared purpose, do you have a diversity of gifts and perspectives on your team?

PRIORITIZING RELATIONAL ACCOUNTABILITY

As we discussed in the previous chapter, accountability is critical for leading together. There are three basic types of accountability (formational, relational, missional), and each type is important when creating a transformative environment. (We explored formational accountability in the previous chapter in reference to spiritual formation.) When talking about environments, the crucial focus is *relational accountability.*

The kind of vulnerability required for formational accountability is limited or even eliminated if we do not create the right kind of relational environment. As noted, Heifetz describes this as a holding environment. From a biblical perspective, though, we want a *covenantal* environment—where there are clear commitments and expectations of one another.

Creating a healthy team covenant is the "secret sauce" of a transforming environment.[30] Throughout Scripture, we see that we follow a God of covenant. For example:

> *Know therefore that the Lord your God is God, the faithful God who maintains covenant loyalty with those who love him and keep his commandments, to a thousand generations.*

Deuteronomy 7:9

Covenant is about *faithfulness* and *loyalty*, and God is always faithful and loyal, no matter how we respond. We see this in various covenants that God made, including covenants with Adam and Eve, with Noah, with Abraham, with Moses, and with David.[31] Even as humans fail, God remains faithful and loyal to us. Ultimately, God demonstrates the depth and breadth of his covenantal love in Jesus.

What if we could operate with one another in the same faithfulness and loyalty that God does with us? Is this not precisely the kind of unity that Jesus prayed for us in John 17? A written, agreed-upon covenant creates the environment for unity amidst our diversity.

Covenant can be a primary means of relational accountability. It clarifies commitment and expectations and encourages faithfulness and loyalty. Keeping such a covenant consistently before us and being accountable to our shared commitments will lead to fruitfulness in our teams.

Earlier we looked briefly at Patrick Lencioni's five dysfunctions of a team: lack of trust, unhealthy conflict, low commitment, avoidance of accountability, and an inattention to results.[32] Conversely, functioning well in these five areas can be seen as marks of a healthy covenantal environment. As an adaptation of Lencioni's work, reflect on these questions and think about a growth scale in each of these five areas:

1. Do we have trust? Is it increasing? Where can it grow or deepen?
2. Are we able to have healthy conflict? Is our adaptive capacity growing?

3. Do we have high commitment to our purpose and to each other? What is impeding it? Do we have competing commitments?

4. Are we accountable to each other for our formation, our relationships, and our mission in Jesus? Specifically in our team, how is our covenant? Are we faithful and loyal to one another based on our agreed-upon commitments and expectations as described in our covenant?

5. Are both our purpose and desired outcomes clear? Is everything we do focused there? Are we making progress?

Imagine what is necessary in your context to have a healthy relational environment. Do you have the courage and discipline to build this into your team?

INCREASING CAPACITY

Creating transformative environments is a way to increase adaptive capacity. This is true because we gain the trust necessary to grow in our ability to do adaptive work, but it is also true because we can truly share purpose with others. This requires letting go of control and giving things away to those on our team—a practice referred to as *delegation*.

Many leaders increase the capacity of their organizations by delegating *tasks* to others. Often these are tasks that the leader does not want to do or is not gifted to do. Delegating tasks carries minimal risk to the leader or organization because the assignment can be rescinded if the task is not fulfilled or is ineffectively executed. Leaders are often reluctant to delegate because they feel a task will be accomplished better "if I just do it myself." As we have already discussed, this type of control is a character trait of the solo-heroic leader. When they do delegate tasks, some leaders cannot keep from micro-managing every little detail, which is disempowering to those they lead. Leaders who effectively learn to delegate tasks will not only increase their own capacities but also the capacities of the organization.

Leaders can also delegate *responsibility*. If someone has proven to be faithful in tasks and trustworthy in character, they may be ready for responsibility. There is often a short leash when giving others tasks to accomplish, but the leash gets a bit longer when delegating responsibility. A proven track record and a trusting relationship between the leader and the person being delegated to are helpful criteria in knowing when to delegate responsibility. For instance, you might have an emerging leader on your team to whom you have assigned tasks. After demonstrating faithfulness with those tasks, you might delegate a leadership responsibility that fits with the emerging leader's gifts, such as leading a Bible study, running a meeting, or even visiting someone in the hospital. As a leader, you watch this emerging leader take responsibility and review their progress. If it goes well, you may trust the person with increasing responsibility over time, while continuing to hold them accountable.

Leaders may also delegate *authority.* If someone has proven responsible and clearly shares your DNA (aligns with your beliefs and purposes), there may come a time where you commission them with authority to lead. You will stay in relationship, but you trust them to lead as if they represent you in every context. I caution leaders not to delegate authority too soon, but I encourage them to build the kinds of relationships and have the kingdom mindset that will enable delegation of authority. This creates the capacity for multiplication.

Jesus clearly taught and delegated in this way throughout the Gospels[33] and early in the book of Acts. He gave his disciples tasks and eventually sent them out with responsibility under his authority. They reported back to him about how their ministry went, and he reminded them to rejoice—not in the results of their efforts, but that their names are written in heaven.[34] Ultimately, he commissioned them to carry his authority into the world and make disciples in his name.[35] We see the multiplying effect of this throughout the book of Acts and beyond.

If delegation is to succeed, a key element is *equipping.* If someone has already been equipped and is trustworthy, you may be able to immediately delegate tasks and even responsibility to them. If an individual is asked to do a task they do not know how to do and no one shows them how to do it, they are more likely to fail and will be hesitant to take the next task. In that scenario, delegation will actually disempower them. If a person is shown what to do, they are more likely to embrace the challenge and learn from the experience—even if it doesn't go perfectly. Certain personality types will jump into a task and figure it out even if they haven't been trained or equipped, but most of us will resist a task for which we are ill-equipped.

Equipping people to do a *task* well is often very technical in nature and is a great place to start in the process of delegation. Equipping people to take on *responsibility* and/or *authority* is a different matter. It takes time and intentionality. It requires a purposeful focus on leadership development. This works well in the context of a team with an emerging leader, where relationships can grow, trust can build, spiritual growth can be observed, and passions and gifts can be discerned and fostered. In this scenario, a leader is equipping and preparing others just as Jesus did with his disciples. This is also how Paul interacted with his various companions in the book of Acts.[36] They were developed as leaders in real-life ministry situations, and, at a certain point, Paul felt the confidence and freedom to send some of them to other places to represent him.

Timothy is a clear example of this. Paul equipped Timothy but also had deep relationship with him; so deep that Paul completely trusted Timothy to lead. Timothy was sent to places with authority to represent the gospel and train and equip others in the same way Paul had done with him. To delegate authority wisely, there must be deep relationship.

My sense is that every follower of Jesus has the capacity to become an equipper. I have interacted with many pastors and seminary students over the last couple of decades who have tremendous leadership capacity but who have yet to grasp their role in developing others. I observed this pattern in one of my former students. He asked the most wonderful reflective questions I had ever heard. He took a course from me in which students experience a "leadership laboratory." After about six months of observing this student, I asked him to train the rest of us (including me) in how to ask questions. He looked at me with confusion and explained he didn't know how to train us; questioning just came naturally to him. He was unconsciously competent.[37] My challenge to him was that he had something he could equip others in if he could figure out how to do so—in other words, I challenged him to become consciously competent. It took some reflection and discernment from him, but, prompted by my encouragement, he finally figured out how to articulate his intuitive process. At that moment, his ability went from *intuitive* to *intentional,* and he discovered how to equip others. I learned something from him that day, and so did my other students.

Equipping takes the right kind of environment and purposeful discernment. We must pay attention to what God has been doing, how it is working, and how to help others do it, too. Most of my students will never be as good as the student who taught them how to ask reflective questions, because he is supernaturally gifted by God with something quite unique. Still, every one of them is now a better questioner because they have been taught. This is the power of an intentional environment of empowering and equipping.

Equipping naturally leads to an environment for mobilization, but once again, this has to be approached intentionally. Mobilizing people is an important piece of leadership. Quoting Heifetz, Bolsinger said, "If 'adaptive leadership is the practice of mobilizing people to tackle tough challenges and thrive,' then if nobody is being mobilized, nobody is being led."[38] This is a profound statement. People have to be equipped if they are to have the confidence to participate in Jesus' mission. But they also have to be mobilized; they have to be allowed to fly. Once people are equipped and empowered by the Spirit, they can take what God has given them and multiply it.

So, what obstacles do you face in creating capacity in others? How can you more effectively delegate tasks, responsibility, and authority? Who is God calling you to intentionally equip? Are they on your team? How can you mobilize your team in a way that can lead to multiplication?

ADOPTING A SIMPLE PATTERN

Creating a strong relational environment lays the groundwork for becoming a healthy team that can overcome adaptive challenges and move faithfully toward God's calling. Having a *pattern* to practice as a team can help facilitate this kind of environment.

For example, I introduced the simple "loving, learning, and leading together" (L3) pattern to SLI. Practically, L3 is a meeting format. Ultimately, though, it is designed to be a way of life that is exercised in order to form a shared culture. It is the environment in which shared purpose and values are articulated, embodied, embedded, and multiplied.[39] This mirrors the environment that Jesus created with his disciples around loving, following, and leading. You may already have a similar pattern. The key question is this: Does our team pattern help people grow in relationship with God and one another as we learn, discern, and experiment together through our adaptive challenges?

Jesus said that our ultimate challenge is loving God with all we are and loving others as we love ourselves.[40] Merely believing in this, or longing for it without observing practices that will make it a reality, will not lead to desired outcomes. It would be like an ensemble of musicians that longs to make beautiful music but never rehearses together. Rather than merely hoping that loving God and others will occur or assuming it will happen at some point, spiritual leaders intentionally create environments that focus first on this greatest commandment. This is L1: loving God and one another.

Within your team's pattern, what intentional practices can you put into place that will help you love God and one another?

The *formational accountability* we discussed in the previous chapter is an example of a practice that helps people grow in our love of God and others.

Another simple practice you might consider is reporting to one another what is referred to as a *glory sighting*—any reminder of God or sense of God's presence or goodness. Somehow, the result of experiencing God's glory is that we move toward the oneness we see in the Trinity. At SLI, we begin meetings and conversations by reminding people of Jesus' prayer in John 17:22, and we ask people to witness to where they have seen God's glory recently. *Where have you had a sense of God's glory, God's goodness, a sense of beauty, a sense of awe?*

This is a simple but incredibly transformative practice. People who are discouraged or even experiencing despair often describe how the environment and their own attitude changes as they hear others share glory sightings and reflect on their own experience of God's glory. Hope rises when people are reminded that God is with us and the challenges we face are small in comparison to God's great grace and glory. The more people share glory sightings, the more their awareness of God grows, and the deeper their experience of trust and camaraderie is with one another. Over time, this practice leads toward the kind of unity that Jesus prayed for and that Paul described as a key element of the church's calling.[41] When people focus on glory sightings regularly, they begin to not only watch for and talk about God's activity in the world, but they also begin to anticipate and participate in God's *present* glory in their own spheres of influence. This is also a simple practice for them to repeat in other spheres, including with their families, neighbors, and coworkers.

Another practice in a healthy team pattern is seeing ourselves as learners. This is L2: learning together. Learning is a value of discipleship and recognizes that we all have growing to do. As it relates to our mission and calling as a team, family, or organization, we are facing adaptive challenges that require the humility to engage every conversation and situation as learners.

From a biblical perspective, our learning is more than fumbling our way forward amid challenges; it is more about *discerning together* (as we saw in Acts 6 and Acts 15). As Ruth Haley Barton says, "We can choose to establish practices that transform us in community. Spiritual community at the leadership level then becomes the context for discerning and doing the will of God, which is the heart of spiritual leadership."[42] Creating the environment that lets us discern and do the will of God together is core to being spiritual leaders. This is what learning together is all about.

Discernment that brings shared learning is facilitated by good questions. Asking the right questions has a powerful influence on an environment because the answers they provide can bring insight, "aha moments," and wisdom—all of which are essential for discernment. We will return to this notion of asking the right questions in even more detail in the next chapter as we look at process practices to consider. It is enough here to mention that effective questions help us in spiritual growth, team relationships, planning, implementation, continual improvement, multiplication, and accountability.

RISKING EXPERIMENTATION

A final element in leading together is taking risks through experimentation. We must foster a safe environment within the team in order to engage together in risky mission. This paradox is necessary because people and teams will seldom move beyond their comfort zone for the sake of the mission if the relationships that hold them are not healthy and safe. In addition, it is the relationships themselves, and the environment within which those relationships exist, that prompts the courage for many to step out in faith. Have you ever noticed that most people are far more courageous in a group than they are alone? Perhaps this is why Jesus sent people out in pairs or in teams. Thus, as we've been discussing throughout this chapter, the right kind of transformative environment is essential if we are to lead in transforming ways together.

The language of "experimentation" is helpful when encouraging risk-taking for the sake of mission—if this experimentation is based on the shared learning and discernment of a team. In other words, we are not advocating for blind risk, but rather suggesting that teams take calculated risks, based on shared calling, values, and convictions.

In reflection, do you have an environment where relationships are safe enough to promote experimentation? Is the fear of failure paralyzing your team? What steps could you take to empower your team toward greater risk-taking and experimentation for the sake of mission?

As with the previous chapter, I have asked many questions throughout this section on practices that are specifically related to creating transformative environments for leading together. Below is a summary of these questions. I invite you to consider these questions for your particular context, and to determine what your most helpful next step is in creating a transformative environment for leading together.

TEAM BUILDING

- Is the purpose of our team clear?
- How has prayer informed our team recruiting?
- Is each person on our team passionate about our shared purpose?
- Do we have a diversity of gifts and perspectives on our team?

RELATIONAL ACCOUNTABILITY

- Do we have trust? Is it increasing? Where can it grow or deepen?
- Are we able to have healthy conflict? Is our adaptive capacity growing?
- Do we have high commitment to our purpose and to each other?
- Are we accountable to clear commitment and expectations?
- Are our purpose and desired outcomes clear?

INCREASING CAPACITY

- What obstacles do we face in creating capacity in others?
- How can we more effectively delegate tasks, responsibility, and authority?
- Who is God calling us to intentionally equip? Are they on our team?
- How can we mobilize our team in a way that leads to multiplication?

ADOPTING A SIMPLE PATTERN

- Does our team pattern help people grow in relationship with God and one another as we learn, discern, and experiment together through our adaptive challenges?
- What pattern could we adopt to help us do so?

EXPERIMENTATION

- Do we have safe enough relationships to promote experimentation?
- Is the fear of failure paralyzing our team?
- What steps could we take to empower our team toward greater risk-taking and experimentation for the sake of mission?

With a healthy team environment in place, we arrive at the final principle of shared spiritual leadership—developing processes that are fruitful.

8

KNOWING THE STANDARDS AND THE FREEDOM TO IMPROVISE: DEVELOPING FRUITFUL PROCESSES

Imagine an exciting jazz number with intricate harmonies, a groovy beat, and remarkable improvised solos. Even if jazz is not your style, perhaps listen to a track, just to get the feel. What enables such beauty and creativity? How are the musicians able to innovate in such novel ways?

In jazz, it is important to know the *standards*. "A 'jazz standard' is a composition that is held in continuing esteem and is commonly used as the basis of jazz arrangements and improvisations."[1] The songs in the canon of jazz standards are musical compositions that are widely known, performed, and listened to … and that have proven over time to be interesting to jazz musicians and improvisers. Composers and performers understand the theory behind the music, which relates to how the music is structured as well as to what is of practical use to improvisers.

> *Of course theory doesn't come close to explaining music. If music is a language, theory is just grammar. More important than grammar is knowing the vocabulary—that comes from listening, with awareness, to great*

players, and playing as much as possible. Beyond grammar and vocabulary is the ability to communicate with listeners—to "tell a story," and to reach an audience on an emotional, or even spiritual, level.[2]

In the first chapter of this book, I described learning to listen. Listening, mimicking, and continual practice are critical in jazz and in growing as spiritual leaders who find creative solutions to adaptive challenges together with others. If jazz has *standards*—which musicians practice, perfect, and then improvise around—what are the *standards* for shared spiritual leadership?

The answer lies in our leadership and in our core processes.

If we want to see fruitfulness, the kind of *leaders* needed in today's world are the ones who lead together with others into uncharted territory. Tod Bolsinger notes, "Even a frame of being an explorer in uncharted territory allows leaders to consider a different way of seeing the challenges in front of them and ask new questions."[3]

We also need a new paradigm for change, which is where *processes* come in. We live in a world that looks for a quick fix to solve difficult challenges, and we serve within a church that is often stuck in a program-driven paradigm. For many churches, and even other types of organizations, this means the solution to most challenges is to simply start a new program. But this is merely a technical solution to an adaptive challenge, and often proves unfruitful. The key is to shift from a *program-driven* paradigm to a *process* paradigm. These most fruitful processes are Spirit-led. As we learn to discern together, both with the Holy Spirit and one another in team, these processes lead to experimentation and ultimately to fruitfulness.

WHY DEVELOP FRUITFUL PROCESSES FOR SHARED LEADERSHIP?

Recall again the *from-through-to* process we discussed in chapter five. Within the adaptive tension and disequilibrium, spiritual leaders create the environment for adaptive leadership to thrive and leverage the *liminal space* between where we've been and where we are called to be. In this "space between," we can increase our adaptive capacity if we continue to learn and find new patterns of interaction. Adaptive leadership is about learning together, and clear *processes* enable healthy learning.

One key reminder is critical here. The emphasis is not on the *processes* themselves but on *fruitfulness.* The processes are simply a means of grace to encounter God and discern with one another. Once we have discerned, they also provide the prompts to move us into action and give us the ability to keep learning and refining our action. Fruitfulness itself is in God's hands and is evidence of the Spirit's activity in our midst. Our role is to develop processes that *bear fruit.* As we discussed previously, we are not *producing* fruit for God but *bearing* fruit in and with God.[4]

To enable us to develop fruitful processes, we will need to adopt two counter-cultural mindsets: a *process view* and a *systems perspective.*

A process view helps us gain clarity on who we are, where we are now, where we are headed together, and how we might close the gap between our current reality and our desired future.

A systems perspective allows us to see the interconnecting components of our environment rather than seeing them as individual and isolated. This viewpoint also helps us realize that transformation can begin anywhere within the environment and grow from there to affect the whole.

With that background, let's look at core processes for fruitfulness.

CORE PROCESSES FOR FRUITFULNESS

Knowing the jazz standards through listening, mimicking, and ongoing practice sets the foundation necessary for improvisation. Once a musician is familiar with the standards, and the chord progressions have become second nature, great jazz musicians alter a composer's original themes through improvisation.[5] Since adaptive leadership also requires learning to improvise and innovate in the context of shared leadership, what processes enable learning that can lead to fruitfulness?

According to Heifetz and his colleagues, there are two core processes of adaptive leadership. They use two helpful metaphors to describe these: *Getting on the balcony* and *getting on the playing field.*[6]

GETTING ON THE BALCONY: SEE AND DISCERN

One of my favorite places on the planet is the Rocky Mountains. I love hiking the trails with my family. I've noticed, though, when I'm in the midst of the trees, it is impossible to see our destination. However, if I can get to a ridge or a clearing, I can gain a new perspective on both where I am going and where I am. And I can also see the terrain between. This is the essence of "getting on the balcony."

When facing adaptive challenges, leaders must resist the instinct to jump into action too quickly.[7] Instead, according to Heifetz, Linsky, and Grashow, getting on the balcony requires that we learn the skills of observation, interpretation, and intervention.[8] This will enable us to see the deeper patterns at work in our ministry or organization. Getting on the balcony allows us to rise above the chaos, truly observe what is going on, and make interpretations about the adaptive challenges we face. In his book *Leadership in a Time of Pandemic,* Bolsinger points out that getting to the balcony provides the "ability to resist default reactions to crises and instead to pause to make as many observations and gather as many interpretations as possible to see the issue at hand in all of its complexities."[9]

From a biblical perspective, getting to the balcony goes beyond mere observation and interpretation. From the balcony, we have the opportunity to *see* and *discern* together. "Jesus said to them, 'Very truly, I tell you, the Son can do nothing on his own, but only what he *sees* the Father doing; for whatever the Father does, the Son does likewise'" (John 5:19, emphasis mine). As we face adaptive challenges, getting on the balcony reminds us to *see* what God is doing and gain his perspective on the context and challenges, as well as reminding us of our calling and destination. The emphasis at this stage is on "seeing not solving."[10]

As we *see* more clearly, the interpretation and intervention steps of getting on the balcony are integrated with *discerning* what seems good to the Holy Spirit and to us.[11] It is not enough to merely make our own interpretations and design interventions; we do that in the context of discernment together with the Holy Spirit and one another. What we see and discern, then, guides us into action on the playing field.

GETTING ON THE PLAYING FIELD: EXPERIMENT AND IMPROVE

The second core process of adaptive leadership is *action*; or, stated metaphorically, *getting on the playing field*. A healthy culture is essential within this process. Individuals only get on the playing field when they feel there is permission and freedom to experiment, innovate, improvise, take risks, and ultimately, to fail. This is why the transforming environments we discussed in the previous chapter are so important: they provide the culture in which risk-taking and innovation can flourish. Especially in our churches, a fear of failure can come from a dangerous theology that links a failed strategy with some sort of sin or disobedience. But failure is an essential part of learning and leading in every other context, so experiencing it in a church setting may simply signal a need to continue to learn.

Experimentation involves improvisation. As Frank Barrett points out, it is in living on the edge of the unknown that there is openness to novelty and an ongoing quest for new alternatives. In experimentation, even small, positive actions can have large consequences, and we can shift to becoming agile and adaptable organizations.[12] This is why even the language of experimentation is refreshing. We are not acting for the purpose of doing something perfectly but instead to test our assumptions and put what we are learning into practice. An openness to experimentation can also foster grace between people in an organization, since it is understood that we are trying something new in order to learn and achieve greater effectiveness in our mission.

Because adaptive leadership is built on learning together, these processes—getting on the balcony and getting on the playing field—are both about learning. And they are iterative (repeating over and over). We begin on the balcony, and then experiment on the playing field. As we experiment, we must return to the balcony to see and discern whether what we are doing is working. As we do so, we gain new insight into how to *improve* our next experiment.

These core processes are both required as we face unchartered territory. Many leaders will jump to action and modify strategies without the critical step of getting to the balcony. Just as often, however, leaders and teams develop plans and strategies that are never implemented. As we practice these processes of adaptive leadership, we increase our adaptive capacity; we continually learn and improve our experiments. Over time, this pattern becomes our "new normal" and leads to a transformed culture in our team and organization. It also provides the potential for a new emergent reality where we have overcome our challenges and have been transformed.

HELPFUL PRACTICES

It is necessary to reiterate the importance of creating a healthy team environment before diving into adaptive conversations. The following are practices designed specifically to operate in a healthy holding environment and can be harmful if implemented outside of it. For instance, discussing conflicting values, naming assumptions, challenging existing culture, clarifying the current reality, and even discussing the effectiveness of strategies demands a certain level of trust and requires an environment that allows for healthy conflict and prioritizes high commitment and accountability to shared outcomes.[13] When healthy team dynamics are absent or low, at best it limits the adaptive capacity of a team, and at worst the conflict could cause irreparable damage both to the relationships and to the organization. This point cannot be overstated.

Assuming you've addressed these concerns, let's look at some helpful practices to facilitate the core processes of getting on the balcony and getting on the playing field.

PRACTICES FOR GETTING ON THE BALCONY: SEE AND DISCERN

On the balcony, we get above the chaos to see and discern together. Referencing this process in a local church, Bolsinger described overcoming adaptive challenges on the balcony this way:

> Adaptive challenges are only going to be solved through new insight into the context, the values and the systemic issues at play in the congregation and within the leaders themselves ... before we can solve any problem, we need to learn to see new possibilities ... seeing those possibilities depends on first seeing ourselves and our congregations as we really are.[14]

Notice the necessity of gaining new insight about the context, values, and systemic issues at play. It is important to have a clear process designed to do just that. In addition, leaders and teams must dream new missional possibilities together and see those in light of their current reality.

The *from-through-to* adaptive leadership process discussed in chapter five is useful here. This process moves *from* the current reality *to* the desired future *through* designing strategies and interventions. It is important to have clarity on the *from* and the *to* before working on the *through*. Discerning and planning on the balcony are keys to effective shared spiritual leadership in this process.[15]

As a preface to walking through the "balcony" process, you might consider inviting your team to share their dreams of holy possibilities. This is a continuation of creating a transforming environment—establishing an atmosphere of hope and reminding us that we are joining Jesus in mission, not just coming up with our own plans. Theologian Walter Brueggemann uses the phrase "prophetic imagination" to describe the role of imagination within a clear picture of the truth of our reality.[16] I'd put it this way: Teams must look honestly at the current reality with a "missional imagination." Our take on reality can discourage us if it is not framed within the possibilities of following a God who can do more than we can imagine.[17]

Dreaming holy possibilities is quite simple: *Ask people to dream out loud about what they imagine could be possible in their context when the kingdom of God shows up on earth as it is in heaven.* I recently asked this question to a new team of leaders in an Anglican congregation. In response, the team shared their dreams of greater unity in their church and community, as well as a picture of ordinary disciples experiencing deep joy as they confidently embody their gifts and share good news with their unbelieving neighbors. These dreams set a tone of hope and gave the team courage to move into honest conversations about their current reality.[18]

CLARIFYING CURRENT REALITY

Have you ever stood in front of one of the giant maps at an airport or a mall? What is the most important part of the map? While some might assume it is the destination, it is actually the "You are Here" dot. This dot is the starting point, much like knowing the key, time signature, and tempo is the starting point for a set of musicians. If musicians are not on the same page on these things, there is no way they can create beautiful music, no matter how talented they are. On an airport map, the directions to your gate are contingent upon knowing where you are starting from—you cannot get directions to somewhere (your destination) from nowhere. Those directions could be radically different depending on your starting point. Although our vision might be clear, it is our current reality that determines how we will move toward that vision.

How do you get a clear picture of your current reality? Your current reality includes the history or narrative of your organization that leads to the present moment. Discovering or clarifying this reality requires deep listening to God, one another, your own organizational citizens or congregants, and your community. This will bring understanding of both the internal dynamics in your organization and the external dynamics in your community or mission field.

Assuming there is a gap between your current reality and your vision, clarifying the current reality can involve difficult conversations that require trust and the ability to stick with the adaptive tension together as a team. This is key in seeing and discerning together with the Spirit.

Other components to consider as you seek to assess the current reality could include demographic research; taking a church or organizational assessment;[19] and diagnosing your greatest adaptive challenges.

Let's take a deeper look at listening and diagnosing your challenges.

Listening. *Listening is the most critical element of clarifying our current reality.* Our first task is to listen to the Lord and try to discern what the Spirit is showing us through what we learn. Creating time and space to listen to the Lord together and share our insights can be helpful. Alternatively, individuals can spend time alone with the Lord and bring back their insights to a team discussion. It is also important to listen to your own organizational citizens or congregants about their dreams and concerns, as well as their perspectives on the greatest opportunities and challenges facing the organization. Rather than holding a townhall meeting that often turns into a debate (or fight), consider a "listening event" where team members merely ask questions and write down responses to discuss later as a team.

Hosting listening sessions with community leaders can also be fruitful, to hear about the greatest opportunities and challenges facing a neighborhood or region. Doing this effectively demonstrates a desire to be engaged in the community. Team members can also be encouraged to do their own interviews in the community to get the perspectives of those who are not in church.

Teams can take the learning from their listening exercises and summarize it with key insights. Summarizing offers another opportunity to *see* and *discern* what is most critical for clarifying current reality.

So, what practices could be most useful for your team to deeply listen to God and one another? How can you listen well to your own congregation and community?

Diagnosing Adaptive Challenges. *How can we demystify our challenges and begin to see how to move forward through them?* One of the most important elements of clarifying current reality is diagnosing our challenges. It is important to remember to look at the challenges systemically rather than taking them personally. This is a helpful reminder both for the leader of a team and for the team itself.

Diagnosing adaptive challenges often begins by simply asking a team to express their perspectives on the issues facing the organization or church. If they have already assessed their current reality, they may also talk about what they gained from that learning. Then it can be helpful to group the challenges into categories. *The Practice of Adaptive Leadership* describes four adaptive challenge archetypes, which might help your team categorize their observations.

1. ***The gap between espoused values and behavior.*** The key here is recognizing that the values operating in reality are different from what we aspire to. For example, we may say we value outreach, but we spend all of our energy and resources internally. Solutions for this will come later. The focus here is simply diagnosis.

2. ***Competing commitments.*** Organizations, just like people, often have multiple commitments that may conflict with one another. This conflict may be revealed when there is not enough budget to support different commitments or when people are frustrated by having to choose to participate or serve in certain areas and not

others. Over time, commitment wanes entirely if this adaptive challenge persists. Diagnosing it here leads to clarifying focus in terms of commitments and priorities.

3. ***Speaking the unspeakable.*** Churches are notorious for having a "culture of nice," in which people avoid talking about hard things. This often reveals a lack of trust and an inability to engage in healthy conflict. It will be impossible to clarify focus and move into experimentation in healthy ways if an environment is not created to speak the unspeakable together.

4. ***Work avoidance.*** Work avoidance is not rooted in laziness, but in avoiding the real challenge in favor of staying busy with what makes us comfortable. An example would be staying busy with worship planning and programming in a church, while avoiding or "brushing under the rug" the inappropriate behavior of a staff member. Work avoidance is a pattern of treating adaptive challenges with technical solutions. It is a reliance on our existing expertise that allows us to feel better about ourselves but does nothing to address the real challenges being faced.[20]

My assumption is that your team's list of challenges connects to one or more of these archetypes. Diagnosing the adaptive challenges is a giant step in clarifying current reality. It can also lead to identifying the organizational systems that perpetuate these very challenges. While this process is difficult and can be painful, it is refreshing to emerge with clarity. With a clear "You Are Here" dot for your current reality, it is possible to *see* and *discern* a pathway forward.

In light of this discussion, what are the primary adaptive challenges you Are facing, and how do they relate to the adaptive challenge archetypes? What insight does this learning bring into clarifying your current reality? How can working through the process of clarifying your current reality bring greater trust and unity in your team?

CLARIFYING FOCUS (VALUES, VISION, MISSION)

Once you've gained clarity on your current reality, where do you focus? Clarifying focus begins with the end in mind. It is *clarity of focus* that enables movement in leaders, teams, and organizations. More specifically, *focus brings impact,* and *impact brings movement.* Like running on a treadmill, without clear focus, activities accomplish little movement toward calling and vision.

It's good to start with the organization's identity statements: values and mission (the organization's core identity), and vision (the desired future).

Many teams and organizations have strong convictions around the articulation of their values, mission, and vision. The process of clarifying focus often begins with taking a deep look at those existing articulations. Ideally our values, mission, and vision are clear and unchanging, although they are certainly refined over time.

Values. *What are the non-negotiable convictions and guiding principles that drive commitment and provide inspiration within our team or organization?* Values determine our decision-making, both personally and organizationally and represent our deepest convictions. Ultimately, deeply held, shared values are a key component of any culture.

Jesus worked with his disciples for three years, primarily embodying and teaching core values. In the Sermon on the Mount,[21] he made it clear that those who embody those values will be blessed. In his discussion of loving both our neighbors and our enemies, Jesus even said, "Be perfect, therefore, as your heavenly Father is perfect" (Matthew 5:48). This seems to indicate that embodying the value of being perfect makes us like the Father. Jesus also used a series of "You heard that it was said … but I say to you" teachings, in which he helped his disciples see the kingdom values beneath behaviors rather than merely looking at the behaviors themselves.[22] When we understand those values, it shapes our behaviors, so we look more like Jesus.

Our behaviors and our decisions come out of our most deeply held values. These values are rooted in our cultural worldview and are often unstated and merely assumed. Unfortunately, there is often a distinct difference between our articulated values and how we live, and it is our actual values and concrete actions that shape our organizations and determine our decisions and priorities. Being clear on your primary preferred values and how those differ from your existing behavior is a critical step in clarifying focus and is crucial to effective shared spiritual leadership. So, what is the distinction between your preferred values and your existing behavior?[23] What assumptions does this reveal? How does this shape your priorities as you seek to close that gap?

Vision. *What are you imagining your future to be?* Vision is a picture of the desired future and is another key component in *clarifying focus*. Vision highlights the gap between where we are now and what God is calling us to in the future, but it only changes the future reality if it compels us to live differently in the present.

Jesus provides an example of vision for us in the first chapter of Acts. When asked about restoring the kingdom, he responds by painting a picture of the future: "But you will receive power when the Holy Spirit has come upon you; and you will be my witnesses in Jerusalem, in all Judea and Samaria, and to the ends of the earth" (Acts 1:8). His disciples felt powerless and afraid, but he helped them see a different vision, in which the gospel would go to the ends of the earth.

In his book *Making Vision Stick,* Andy Stanley offers a helpful guide to casting vision that is also useful for developing vision in a team. He asks four basic questions:

1. What is the problem?
2. What is the solution?
3. Why us?
4. Why now?[24]

Mission. *Why do we exist?* The final component of *clarifying focus* is having a clear mission or purpose. As Bolsinger said, "The first component of developing adaptive capacity is to realize that it's a process of learning and adapting to fulfill a missional purpose, not to fix the immediate issues."[25] In our discussion in the previous chapter on building teams, I emphasized the importance of having a clear purpose before even beginning a team. Whilst the purpose that brought the team together around shared passions is the starting point, the team may now begin to articulate and own a different purpose.

Mission connotes action. With this in mind, think about how you could describe your primary sense of mission by using a series of action verbs arranged in a sequence of stages. For many local churches and church plants, the mission likely connects to making disciples of Jesus, given his own words in the Great Commission[26]—but expressing that in action verbs is common. For example, we have seen churches utilize verbs such as *know, grow, go;* or *engage, relate, equip, send;* or *win, build, equip, multiply;* or *seek, connect, grow, become.* For other types of organizations, the purpose may be different, but the process still works. As another example, SLI's mission is to *discover, develop,* and *deploy* passionate spiritual leaders. Based in your sense of purpose, what verbs describe your mission in a sequence of stages? If you live out those verbs repeatedly, will you accomplish your mission over time? How does clarity of focus bring greater energy and momentum to your team?

With clarity of *current reality* and clarity of *focus,* we are now ready to start imagining how to move forward. In Heifetz's terms, we have done observation and interpretation on the balcony, and now we are ready to design interventions to get on the playing field.

SYSTEMS AND STRATEGIES

How do we intentionally do something to move in the direction God is calling us? Built on the foundation of our values and mission, we refine our systems and implement our strategies.

Hopefully it has been clear how we are *seeing* and *discerning* on the balcony in clarifying current reality and focus. It is critical that we continue to *see* and *discern* from the balcony as we design systems and strategies rather than merely coming up with our own ideas. The question here is this: as the Spirit leads us from here, how will we embody our values, accomplish our mission, and reach our vision?

It is common for many churches to attempt to close the gap between their current reality and vision with programs. Most church programs are actually designed to help with disciple-making in some way, but they are seldom connected together in a way that bears that kind of fruit. This is where a *systems perspective* can serve us well. Systems are interrelated and interdependent parts that work together as a whole, producing an outcome that is greater than the sum of the parts. We see this in the human body and the wonder of its various systems that work together to help us thrive. God has also built systems into nature. These can be described as generative systems because reproduction is built into their design. In a tree, for example, we see seed, then sprout, then sapling, then fruit; and in the fruit is the seed for yet another tree. Amazingly, each seed has the capacity to bear not only another tree but a forest. We want to likewise develop systems that are generative in their design.

In designing systems, it is critical to remember that this is a team effort, and systems must be designed to embody, embed, and multiply our articulated values, vision, and mission. Within systems, strategies are the specific activities designed to bring about a particular outcome. Systems are refined over time, and strategies can be constantly adjusted based on our learning.

A number of years ago, I was coaching a congregation that had been facing difficult adaptive challenges with a solo-heroic leader at the helm. I helped the pastor build what became a marvelous team with a healthy environment. They were embodying a flourishing relational atmosphere with a strong covenant, and they had done the balcony work of clarifying current reality and focus. One particular Saturday morning, "designing a disciple-making system" was on the team meeting agenda. There was a young man on their team who was called into his regular job and was therefore unable to attend the meeting. He was reluctant to miss it because of his covenant commitment, but the team was gracious to him in light of his circumstance.

This young man's absence created an opportunity for me to paint the picture to the rest of the team of the power of a generative system. You see, he had become a follower of Jesus in this church after going through a painful divorce in his early twenties. Not only had he started a journey with Jesus in this church, but he had also grown in faith, been equipped to lead, and had initiated a new ministry with other young adults. He had become a disciple-making disciple. I reminded the team of this young man's story, and, like proud parents and grandparents, their faces lit up as they remembered God's work in him within their environment. I then posed this question: "It is clear that he has become a disciple-making disciple—so, how did it happen?"

They had no answer except to call it a miracle and give the glory to God. Certainly, it was God's work, and God alone deserved the glory. But in asking my question, I was assuming something intentional had happened that the Spirit used to bring this transformation. In other words, I assumed that God transformed him, but there was some kind of human participation from the church in terms of the environment and the process. Upon a bit more digging, we discovered that a couple in the church had invited this young man into their home in the midst of his pain. They fed him, loved him, and eventually led him into relationship with Jesus. They brought him to church gatherings, introduced him to others, and helped disciple and equip him. They also encouraged him to follow God's call on his life.

The discovery for the team was that this miracle happened in an intentional environment with an intentional process, but it was not something the church as a whole had done intentionally. It happened because of the faithfulness of an individual Christian family—who didn't want any credit and were even embarrassed by being "found out." Seeing their friend become a disciple-making disciple was the fruit this family wanted to see, and it happened miraculously through their work. This example provided the impetus for the team to develop an intentional disciple-making system in order to purposefully focus on their mission and see multiplied fruitfulness over time.

As you reflect on the verbs you use to describe your mission, how could you develop a repeating system around those stages? Where would you place your existing strategies in those system stages? Where are your gaps? What experiments might tackle these gaps? How can designing systems and strategies strengthen your team and prompt action in your organization?

PRACTICES FOR GETTING ON THE PLAYING FIELD: EXPERIMENT AND IMPROVE

The playing field is where we move from learning together to leading together. We must put what we are discerning into action through experimentation and continual improvement. Experimentation is critical because it is "the key to surviving in a changing world."[27] What is your process for experimentation and continual improvement? How are you accountable to your mission?

We discussed formational and relational accountability in the previous chapters. The third type of accountability is *missional accountability*. *Missional accountability,* just like the formational and relational accountabilities already discussed, requires a rhythm and cadence in order for it to become effective and fruitful.

I hear pastors and other church leaders often say that it is difficult, if not impossible, to hold ordinary people accountable for participating in the mission of Jesus through a local church or ministry. It often feels as if the only solution is to hire people as staff in order to get them into mission. If this is our only strategy, though, we will have a minimal kingdom impact.

The alternative is to develop an intentional process to solve the problem.

When we design systems to deal with our challenges, we need to use our imaginations—and we need to see these systems as experimental, Typically, these designs are merely prototypes that need to be tested and refined. While the team will have discussed multiple potential experiments, an important step toward shared spiritual leadership is to prioritize and launch a first experiment. Setting priority comes in prayer and conversation, along with determining what experiment best meets the need and is something that the team can actually do.[28]

One church I was coaching had a gap in their system of outreach. One of their values pointed to relational witness, and many people outside the church in their context were skeptical—even resistant—to events in the church building. They imagined many potential experiments, but ultimately prioritized and designed a single experiment that would equip some families in the church to host neighbors in their homes to build relationships and invite conversation about faith. The strategy itself was built upon a simple process they called "invite, eat, share, pray."[29] They began with one family inviting neighbors to their home to watch a game and eat together (which is quite different from starting a church-wide program everyone is expected to join). They learned from the prototype that neighbors appreciated an invitation to a meal, although other pieces of their process needed thought and improvement. After refining their strategy, they equipped several other families to do the same.

Once an experiment is prioritized, accountability to take the risk of launching the new strategy is critical. We must name what we are going to "do" and name who will take that step. In the example above, one member of the leadership team committed his family to the first experiment.

Once a new experiment is launched, a process like RAD helps us refine and improve our strategies. RAD (Reflect-Adjust-Do) is the process SLI uses for experimentation and continual improvement and to ensure *missional accountability.* While you may utilize different language, this process helps leaders and teams move into action on the playing field but also helps them continue to learn as they experiment.

Being on the field allows what some refer to as *action learning.* Only once we are doing something can we reflect upon that action and adjust it for greater effectiveness. RAD embeds discernment into our experiments. I like to describe the RAD process as a corporate iteration of sanctification. People often associate sanctification with what the Holy Spirit is doing in us individually to transform us to become more like Jesus. I also see sanctification in the larger picture of the Holy Spirit's work in us as a community to enable us to embody the kingdom of God in more faithful and fruitful ways. Working toward "continual improvement" can imply that *we* are driving the changes, whereas using RAD as a corporate sanctification process helps us remember that the *Holy Spirit* is the real change agent, and we are participating with what the Spirit is doing.

Here is a key phrase to consider: Getting it "right" is secondary to getting started and continuing to improve! Tim Brown, CEO at IDEO, said: "Don't think of it as failure, think of it as designing experiments through which you are going to learn …. Failure is an inherent part of the process because we'll just never get it right on our first try."[30]

One of my favorite examples of this is in the Disney animated movie *Meet the Robinsons.*[31] Lewis, the protagonist, is an orphan and an aspiring twelve-year-old inventor. His inventions always seem to *almost* work but continue to fail one way or another. Desperate to be part of a family, his eccentricity scares off many potential parents. Lewis ends up in the future where he meets his family-to-be, and to his delight, it turns out they are using one of his future inventions. But his excitement quickly turns to disappointment when the invention malfunctions, and he once again feels like a failure. But rather than chastise him, the family cheers for his failure. His crazy future aunt simply tells him, "From failure we learn; from success—not so much." From this, his life motto emerges: "Keep moving forward."

Many leaders and teams become paralyzed at the thought of attempting an experiment because they are afraid to fail. We must have the courage to risk together in team with the assumption that we may fail our way forward in the process of learning. We have to start somewhere and then "keep moving forward." We want our experiment design to be as well thought-through as possible, but we also know that the greatest learning will come once we are on the playing field in action.

A process like RAD can help us personally answer and be accountable to the "how is it with your soul?" question, and RAD can also help us be accountable with the "how is it with our mission?" question. It is important to embed a process like this in each team meeting once experimentation has begun. Here are some typical RAD questions/tasks:

- Reflect
  - o What's our goal with this experiment?
  - o What's our plan?
  - o How is it working and why?
- Adjust
  - o What are we going to do differently?
  - o Consider and discern options for improvement.
- Do
  - o Who's going to do what and by when?
  - o Track the results.

While this is a simple process, when there is true accountability and it becomes a cadence for a team during experimentation, it accelerates learning and improves action. This process also enables us to be accountable to putting prioritized experiments into action to overcome our challenges en route to what God has called us to become together.

THE POWER OF THE QUESTION

Moving courageously together through our challenges into new territory requires a particular kind of spiritual leadership, an environment for transformation, and processes that move us from where we are to where God has called us to be. Bolsinger describes it this way: "Exploration challenges the expert expectation …. I encourage leaders to escape the expert expectation by becoming an expert experimenter, an expert question asker instead of answer giver."[32] Bolsinger continues by indicating that asking great questions brings more than mere solutions but can actually lead to transformation. Transformation is our ultimate goal—that we be more like Jesus and that we better mirror his kingdom on earth. As I hope you have grasped, one of our greatest tools of shared spiritual leadership is the power of the question.

Jesus was an expert question-asker. He asked more than three hundred questions in the Gospels that created the environment for conversation, engagement, discovery, and critical thinking. He even answered questions that others asked him with another question. There is power in Jesus' questions, both to create a particular kind of transformative environment and to invite people into a journey of discovery with him.

In his book *A More Beautiful Question,* Warren Berger says, "A beautiful question is an ambitious yet actionable question that can begin to shift the way we perceive or think about something—and that might serve as a catalyst to bring about change."[33] In an environment of shared spiritual leadership, powerful questions can be one of our most valuable tools. The key is asking the right questions that guide people through a process of discernment and transformation. This discernment leads to clarity, which can help us both own our story and calling, but—like playing beautiful jazz music for an audience—it also helps us communicate our story and calling to others.

Below is a summary of some of the questions we have looked at in this chapter.

FROM: CLARIFYING CURRENT REALITY

- What practices are most useful for our team to deeply listen to God and one another?
- How can we listen well to our own congregation and community?
- What is/are the primary adaptive challenge(s) we are facing?
- What insight does this learning bring into clarifying our current reality?

TO: CLARIFYING FOCUS

- What is the distinction between our preferred values and our existing behavior? What assumptions does this reveal? How does this shape our priorities as we seek to close that gap?
- What are we imagining our future to be? What is the problem? What is the solution? Why us? Why now?
- Why do we exist? What verbs describe our mission in a sequence of stages? If we embody those verbs repeatedly, will we accomplish our mission over time?
- How does clarity of focus bring greater energy and momentum to our team?

THROUGH: SYSTEMS & STRATEGIES

- As the Spirit leads, how will we embody our values, accomplish our mission, and reach our vision?
- How could we develop a repeating system around mission stages?
- Where would we place our existing strategies in those system stages?
- Where are our gaps? What experiments might tackle these gaps?
- How can designing systems and strategies strengthen our team and prompt action in our church or organization?

IMPROVE: RISKING EXPERIMENTATION

- What is our process for experimentation and continual improvement?
- How are we accountable to our mission?
- How does experimentation embolden our team and church or organization?

As we draw this section on principles and practices to a close, I invite you to picture again the power of leading together. Consider questions that help develop relationships in team, that help people grow spiritually, that help teams see and discern on the balcony, and that bring accountability to teams experimenting on the playing field. Embodying these principles has the potential to bring true discernment and ultimately leads to fruitfulness.

ENCORE

In 2003, General Stanley McChrystal was tasked with defeating Al-Qaeda in Iraq. Because Al-Qaeda was a fundamentally different kind of enemy from anything the US had previously faced, to conquer them required a transformation of the US Joint Special Operations Task Force. The task force had its own organizational DNA of policies, hierarchy, and siloed thinking. They needed to be able to learn at a pace that kept up with their rapidly changing and complex challenges. The standard operating procedures were "far too slow to be effective," so they had to change their approach to a more integrated and collaborative effort, described by the General as a "team of teams." Their new approach embodied some simple, yet radically different practices, which transformed their culture. Such practices included commitment to shared outcomes, framing powerful questions, reflecting more to learn faster, maximizing the potential for friction, eliminating unproductive friction, and a bias toward action.[1] They clearly learned the way of adaptive shared leadership.

The adaptive challenges the church faces today are like a new kind of enemy. Our world has been through a tsunami of change in the past few years, including a global pandemic, technological advances, as well as increased political and sociological polarization. Many of us assume that what our organizations need is leaders who already know the answers and who can clearly articulate where to go—so the rest of us can simply follow. This is the paradigm of solo-heroic leadership.

But we must adapt our way of leading if we have any hope of getting to the other side of our greatest adaptive challenges. The task is great, but if transformation was possible within the Joint Special Operations Task

Force—a politically charged, hierarchical culture—how much more is it possible within the church, as together we are led by the Holy Spirit in Christ Jesus to the glory of God?

Remember the picture of the beautiful, improvisational movements of a synchronized group of starlings. In response to their ever-changing context, they move together like a dance or a chorus. This shared movement is referred to as a "murmuration," because of the sound produced by multiple wingbeats. Like a symphony, the birds are literally *sounding together.* According to 3D reconstructions, each starling moves and interacts with its closest six to seven neighbors within the larger flock.[2] This makes them a team of teams. If birds can change, shape, and innovate together, surely we can learn to do the same.

My desire for this book is less about learning to follow particular practices and more about highlighting the paradigm of shared spiritual leadership and providing a framework and set of principles that can guide your leadership in the face of change.

As you finish reading this book, take some time to think about your own leadership context. Are you functioning more as a solo-heroic leader with struggles around control, insecurity, ego, or lack of repeatability? What would it take to move toward leading together in ways that are empowering and generative? Are you learning to listen to the Lord and others around you? Is the Holy Spirit inviting you into deep change that moves you to more intimate union with Jesus, the emptying of self through kenosis, and a more faithful embodiment of your own identity and calling as a spiritual leader?

If you have a team, are you truly equipping each person to become a spiritual leader? Do you model the way for them? Is the environment you have created conducive to both their transformation in Christ and to shared discernment through your greatest challenges? Are you experiencing harmony and unity? Do you have processes in place that enable each team member's formation and shared discernment such that you can experiment together toward a new reality and calling? Is there synergy as you lead together? Do you have ways to be accountable for spiritual growth, relational health, and missional engagement? Do the spiritual leaders you are equipping have the confidence and competence to develop more spiritual leaders? Have you designed systems that can multiply? Can you continue to grow and improve together to resemble the kingdom of heaven more faithfully and fruitfully? Are you experiencing freedom and joy together?

Throughout the pages of this book, we have focused our attention on the leadership paradigm shift that moves us *from* solo-heroic leadership *to* generative team leadership. This leads us *through* the real adaptive challenges we are facing *toward* the multiplication of spiritual leaders and organic teams into movement. This shift includes the necessary dynamics of empowerment (vs. control), creating intentional environments and processes (vs. intuitive or haphazard ones), trusting in God and others (vs. trusting my own intellect), participating together (vs. passivity), overcoming adaptive challenges (vs. being overwhelmed), interdependence (vs. isolation or independence), and joyful fruitfulness (vs. being stuck).

What would it look like and how would it affect others around us if we experienced the complete joy of Jesus? Throughout this book, we have discussed the words of Jesus in John 15: "I have said these things to you so that my joy may be in you, and that your joy may be complete" (John 15:11). Through more than two decades of coaching leaders amid their adaptive challenges, I have recognized that *experiencing joy together* is a mark of fruitfulness in followers of Jesus who are leading together, in love, toward a shared purpose.

It really is possible for you to experience these things. Take a deep breath and be reminded that the transformation you desire is in God's hands, not yours. However, it will not happen accidentally; it will come as you abide in him individually and with others. Ask the Lord to give you imagination for the holy possibilities of shared purpose and a shared life of love with others. Remember that even the greatest obstacles in our path can be overcome together with God and one another, for God is able to do more than we can ask or imagine.[3] Just take a step; God will meet you in grace, and you can know the freedom and joy of leading together with others.

If you haven't already, join the adventure of shared spiritual leadership.

Move away *from* solo-heroic, technical leadership that is inadequate for today's world.

Move *to* generative, shared, missional leading together.

Do so *through* building adaptive capacity into your team and organization.

Take the plunge into deep change and embody abiding, humility, and courage.

And may you see God's kingdom come in your midst.

APPENDIX A: BUILDING HEALTHY TEAMS

Part three of this book pointed to helpful practices to achieve shared spiritual leadership. Here is some additional detail related specifically to building healthy teams. There is far more entailed in leading teams and organizations through adaptive change, but that is beyond the scope of this book and will be addressed in future material.

If you have questions or are interested in additional resources, please reach out to me at www.bryandsims.com or to Spiritual Leadership, Inc. (SLI) at www.spiritual-leadership.org.

BUILDING HEALTHY TEAMS

Building a healthy team is a critical practice for creating environments that foster transformation. There is a clear assumption throughout this book that a *team* is necessary to overcome adaptive challenges and more effectively and fruitfully fulfill the purpose to which God has called us. So how is a healthy team built?

- Begin with *clear purpose*
- Select the *right leader*
- Recruit the *right team members*
- Build in *healthy DNA*
- Establish *clarity*

Building a team begins with a *clear purpose.*

It's important to have clarity around the team's "why." While people may initially commit to a leader, without a clear shared purpose, they are unlikely to stay.

Along with clear purpose, a team must have the *right leader.*

It may be assumed that a person fills this spot because of their position or role, but it is key to find a person with deep passion and a calling for the mission with the gifts, skills, maturity, and experience to lead.

With clarity of purpose and the right leader, it is now critical to recruit the *right team members.*

Jesus spent the night in prayer prior to recruiting his own team,[1] and prayer should be the starting point for us, too. Next, assuming shared purpose (which is essential), identify what gifts, perspectives, strengths, and skills most complement the leader of the team.[2] Only once those complementary gifts, perspectives, and skills have been considered can you begin to think who might be suitable. And don't forget that diversity on a team will lead to greater impact and effectiveness.

Now the team leader needs a script for recruiting team members, which should include the team purpose and commitment expectations, along with the reason each person is being invited. Too many leaders apologize when asking for a team commitment because they know people are busy. (As we discussed throughout the book, this is often actually more about our own insecurities than our concern for people.) Rather than apologizing, invite people into something with great value that connects with their passions and sense of purpose.

Once team members are recruited, it is critical for the team to be built on *healthy DNA.*

For SLI, this means requiring a commitment to practicing Loving, Learning, and Leading (L3) as a way of life, creating and adhering to a team covenant (see Appendix B), establishing practices that help us grow as spiritual leaders (see Appendix C), and discerning how the Holy Spirit will lead us through our greatest adaptive challenges toward the purpose and vision of the team.

Finally, it is important for the team to function with *clarity*.
Establishing clarity begins with being specific about meeting schedule and regularity. SLI insists that teams meet for at least eight hours per month for a minimum of a year. This allows the time to practice L3 without rushing the formational, relational, or missional priorities. (Your time frame may be different.)

For individuals to be committed, they must put the team meetings on their calendars. We encourage teams to set the meeting schedule for the entire year. If adjustments are needed along the way, the team can discuss this and make modifications.

Planning the opening meeting is also essential for establishing clarity and starting strong. Whenever possible, we encourage retreats for opening sessions, which allows people to get away and enjoy building relationship with one another, worshiping together, and beginning their team process with high commitment.

APPENDIX B: CREATING A STRONG TEAM COVENANT

Part three of this book pointed to helpful practices to achieve shared spiritual leadership. Here is some additional detail related specifically to building a strong team covenant.

If you have questions or are interested in additional resources, please reach out to me at www.bryandsims.com or to Spiritual Leadership, Inc. (SLI) at www.spiritual-leadership.org.

CREATING A STRONG TEAM COVENANT

Rather than having a team leader dictate covenantal commitments and expectations to a team, there is great power in giving team members a role (and thus ownership) in this process.

SLI uses four questions to guide the process of building a covenant that will work for any type of team. (For a sample covenant, see the end of this section.)

1. What are the characteristics of great leaders?
2. What are the characteristics of great teams?
3. What are our team non-negotiables?
4. How will we refine our non-negotiables into a team covenant?

SLI assumes that the members of teams will become spiritual leaders over time, so there is both a spiritual-leader emphasis and a team emphasis here.

Given these emphases, the ***opening two questions*** in our covenant-building process focus on the ideal by asking people to think about the characteristics of great leaders and great teams. Brainstorming these questions encourages dynamic team interaction, which is key for adaptive leadership. We simply ask these questions and then take notes on a white board while a team throws out every idea that comes to mind. Typically, these opening questions net long lists of potential characteristics that seed the next question.

Question three focuses on identifying team non-negotiables. This question invites critical thinking and discernment around what individuals are willing to commit themselves to. I often introduce it like this: "This is the only point in the entire adaptive leadership process where I encourage you to be selfish. I want you to think about your own personal non-negotiables that would enable you to be "all in" with your commitment to this team and purpose. They may come from your own convictions of what you desire, or they may result from previous hurts or betrayals. Either way, write down your own non-negotiables."

Once each person has written down their personal non-negotiables, each is invited to share those with the team. There are often striking similarities in what is shared, and this vulnerability of sharing fosters trust. We again simply capture this list of non-negotiables on a white board.

The ***final question/step*** to building covenant is to refine those non-negotiables into clear commitments that the team can be accountable to. This often begins by grouping the non-negotiables into categories of three to five larger ideas. Then we make sure to clearly define each category and specify how we will be accountable to it. Some groups do this in simple bullet points while others craft more of a short narrative. One example of a category would be "love and respect for one another," under which one of the bullet points could be "confidentiality." Confidentiality must be clearly defined, so a group might decide on something like "keeping personal sharing in the group." Not everything in a team will be confidential, so it is important to determine what must be kept within the group in such a way that the team has clear commitment and expectations. (See the sample covenant.)

Building a covenant can create the environment for healthy relationships, but the key is *relational accountability*. Because of this, the covenant must be reviewed in each meeting. This review is often merely a brief check-in to make sure all hearts are clear. The check-in is also an opportunity for deeper sharing and even confession that deepens trust and commitment. If covenant is ignored, over time the commitment of a team will wane. If covenant is broken, this objective written document gives the team a way to have hard conversations. If covenant is kept, over time the team will grow into greater interdependence and unity.

When people are working together, it is common for relational conflicts to emerge. When there are differing expectations or values on the team, this can erode into dysfunction. As we have discussed, having a clear and shared purpose is critical in forming a team. However, even with shared purpose, conflict can arise. This is precisely why we form covenant together in the opening team session, because the importance of a healthy environment cannot be overstated. When we have a clear covenant that articulates our shared commitment and expectations, then the covenant itself can be used to navigate our relational conflicts. For instance, when conflict arises, we can look together at the covenant we have created to help us discern how to proceed. Rather than subjectivity, the covenant provides a lens to objectively review our interactions with one another. If they are well facilitated, these conflict conversations can serve to develop deeper trust, respect, and understanding as teams discuss what might have otherwise been undiscussable. The covenant, in this case, keeps us from a mere "culture of nice" and instead gives us boundaries and guidelines for how to speak the truth in love. Doing this well takes practice, and sometimes the help of a coach or facilitator can be beneficial. However, the covenant reminds us of the promises we have made to one another and helps us keep those commitments.

SAMPLE COVENANT

We want to be a church that purposefully glorifies Christ together and in the surrounding community. To do this we adopt the following commitments and practices:

- Live in freedom and grace, as individuals and as a congregation.
- Generate new church ministries.
- Hold each other accountable in our personal discipleship.

In support of these commitments and practices, we make these covenants:

Prayer

- Focus on a specific prayer need as a team each session
- Pray weekly for other group members as, together, we seek God's leading and direction

Presence

- Commit to full engagement in the process by attending every session, notifying members in case of an absence
- Offer grace and trust to each other
- Complete homework prior to attending team meetings
- Begin and end meetings on time

Confidentiality

- Use discretion when sharing details from team discussions
- Keep confidential all personal concerns and accountability plans
- Refrain from intentionally saying words that could hurt or be perceived as hurtful

Throughout the journey we commit to:

- Encourage each other
- Celebrate all accomplishments, big or small, personal or congregational
- Enjoy the journey of growth on which God has called us

This document should be used as a sample; it contains only general ideas of what a Covenant could look like.

APPENDIX C: FACILITATING SPIRITUAL GROWTH IN TEAMS

Part three of this book pointed to helpful practices in achieving shared spiritual leadership. Here is some additional detail related specifically to facilitating spiritual growth in teams.

If you have questions or are interested in additional resources, please reach out to me at www.bryandsims.com or to Spiritual Leadership, Inc. (SLI) at www.spiritual-leadership.org.

FACILITATING GROWTH THROUGH TEAM SPIRITUAL FORMATION

The concept of "spiritual formation" acknowledges that only the Holy Spirit transforms us[1] and that God often transforms us amid trusting relationships with others. Thus, we want to create an environment that fosters the Holy Spirit's work in us within community. Chapter six mentions *glory sightings* as a helpful practice to create a transforming environment in team meetings, as we are reminded of God's activity in, around, and through us. We also constantly acknowledge that fruitfulness comes only as we abide in Jesus as he abides in us, since apart from him we can do nothing.[2] What are some other practices that facilitate spiritual growth in our teams?

In his book *Invitation to a Journey*, Robert Mulholland describes "spiritual formation as (1) a process (2) of being conformed (3) to the image of Christ (4) for the sake of others."[3] We help create an environment that fosters spiritual formation and growth when we have an *intentional process* for being conformed into the image of Christ. Inherent in this definition is the reminder that we are bearing fruit "for the sake of others" and not for ourselves. The critical practice needed here is *accountability* for such growth. In other words, we need an environment and intentional processes for purposeful accountability in relationships. Most of us have convictions about what the Lord wants for us as a next step, but we seldom grow consistently without these accountable relationships. This is why we need *formational accountability.*

In practice, formational accountability looks like people asking specific questions of one another on a regular basis (weekly, as a recommendation) for the purpose of growth. We often begin this conversation by asking people to **share how they best connect with God**. For example, some will share about how they connect with God best through music, others through study, others in groups, and still others in nature or in prayer. The point of this first question is to remind people that we are all wired differently. We all connect with God in Christ through the Holy Spirit, but we do so in a variety of ways. This illustrates the creativity of God but also keeps people from assuming a "one-size-fits-all" approach to spiritual growth.

Having shared about how we best connect to God, we invite people to ask the Holy Spirit to reveal a clear next step in response to this question: **What action(s) do I intend to take to help me more fully abide in Jesus?** We often encourage people to pause and listen for a few moments and write down one thing the Spirit reveals to them. After those moments of silence, we invite the team members to share what they heard (their accountability prompts). Each subsequent week when they meet, they share about how they are doing with those prompts and solicit accountability for each new next step as the Spirit continues to lead.[4]

It is important to note here that many people have experienced accountability, whether in church or another setting, as "shaming" in some way. This unfortunate reality makes it critical to create a safe and healthy environment for spiritual formation. A few simple guidelines, shared in an opening meeting together, help make this possible:

- Only the Holy Spirit can bring transformation.
- We are not here to fix each other (no offering advice).
- Show respect for every individual in the group.
- Answer in first person.
- Write down team members' requests for prayer and accountability.
- Leaders are called to apply gentle yet firm means of accountability.

We have already described the first point, above, in detail throughout this book: ***Only the Holy Spirit can bring transformation.*** Only God transforms us. We do not transform others, just as we do not transform ourselves. As Paul said, "And all of us, with unveiled faces, seeing the glory of the Lord as though reflected in a mirror, are *being transformed* into the same image from one degree of glory to another; for this comes from the Lord, the Spirit" (2 Corinthians 3:18, emphasis mine). Notice that we are seeing God's glory (glory sightings) and *being transformed* from glory to glory by the Spirit.

We can trust that the Holy Spirit will transform us to become more like Jesus, so we must acknowledge that ***we are not here to fix each other***—as tempting as that might be. Some of us are "fixers" by personality, some of us lean this way simply out of concern and empathy for what others are experiencing. There are some, though, whose attempt to fix others reveals their own insecurities. An insecure person will always be driven to provide answers and fix people's problems. For those of us like this, everything comes back to our security and identity needing to be in the Lord. We must learn to trust that others, just like us, are the Lord's beloved and that the Lord is able to work in them without our help.

This desire or need to fix others often leads us to give advice or attempt to counsel people as they share. For instance, as someone shares in a team about a struggle they have, the "fixer" immediately remembers a similar experience and shares it in an attempt to help. Unfortunately, even if the intent is to help, those who receive unsolicited advice are often hurt by it. In fact, gurus in spiritual formation, as well as those who research the psychological and emotional dynamics of group interactions, use the language of violence to describe how people experience being "fixed." We must therefore avoid these temptations. Leaders must articulate guidelines and watch for any attempt to fix, as it can damage both people within a group and the group itself.[5]

By trusting the Holy Spirit's work in one another and avoiding the temptation to fix, we can *show respect for every individual in the group*. Ultimately, this guideline is a reminder that we are all made in the image of God, which gives us eternal value. Respecting one another in this way allows us to embody the kind of spiritual leadership that has already been described through this book.

The next bullet indicates that we will *answer in first person*. It is impossible to be held accountable for something we want someone else to do. For example, a pastor may name that what he really needs is for his staff to do something. A denominational leader may say, "If I could just get those pastors to…" A husband may say, "If my wife would only…" The guideline of answering in first person is a reminder that we must reflect with the Holy Spirit on what *we* are being called to do and ask for accountability around something *we* have some measure of control over in our own lives.

Next, we *write down requests for prayer and accountability*. We do this for at least three reasons. First, writing down team members' requests helps us remember. If we are going to hold one another accountable, we must remember what those requests are so that we can pray and ask one another in subsequent meetings about our progress in grace. Second, writing things down conveys value to the one speaking. If I record what you are sharing, I show you that I am listening and care about you; that you are important to me and to us as a team. Third, recording these items prevents people from interrupting one another or not fully listening. Writing things down invites the whole team to lock in on what is being shared with each person and keeps us from interrupting or ignoring one another.

Finally, *leaders are called to apply gentle yet firm means of accountability*. This final guideline reminds us that true accountability requires both the gentleness that is a fruit of the Spirit and the ability to truly lean into the challenges together. Grace meets us right where we are but loves too much to let us stay there. We each have value just because of who we are in Christ, but we are also provoked to grow more deeply into the image of Christ.

In addition to the above-mentioned steps of *formational accountability* (sharing how they best connect with God and what actions they intend to take to more fully abide in Jesus), teams will often *worship together, share*

Scripture with one another, and *choose a shared devotional pattern or process to follow* on a daily basis. When doing so, these teams will share reflections from their daily times of prayer and Scripture reading as part of their regular team meetings.[6] As we discussed previously, the point of these patterns is practicing the means of grace. Ultimately, the aim of creating space for worship and conversation around Scripture is to respond to God's grace, mercy, and love with worship and surrender, which will lead to us becoming more and more like the One we worship. A byproduct of all these practices of spiritual formation is deepened relationship and trust in the team.

Finally, to create an environment that fosters transformation, it is crucial to *pray together.* If we truly believe that only God brings transformation and that fruitfulness comes as we abide in Jesus, then prayer must be a practice that is more than a bookend to each meeting. We want all our interactions to be bathed in prayer and for even our conversations with one another to be prayerful. In practical terms, this means we have times of focused prayer and specific intercession for the team and for one another, but also for the mission God has called us to and for those we are called to serve.

One of my favorite quotes on prayer is from John Wesley, who said, "Whether we think of or speak to God; whether we act or suffer for him; all is prayer when we have no other object than his love, and the desire of pleasing him."[7] We often ask teams how they define prayer and why prayer is important. Then we ask them to reflect on Wesley's definition and its implications. Wesley seemed to think that everything could be prayer if the love of God was inherent within it. What does that mean for every aspect of our work when we are facing adaptive challenges? It means that focused and dedicated prayer is critical if we are to see the fruitfulness we long to see. I believe that even our conversations with one another can be a form of prayer if we are seeking God and discerning what seems good to the Holy Spirit and to us. I say this because I have witnessed the Holy Spirit working during a conversation among team members where there is unity of purpose and love, which results in holy "ahas" that lead to fruitfulness.

It is also crucial that prayer for one another and for the mission and community are intentionally integrated into the team covenant. (See Appendix B.) As part of this covenant commitment, teams often pray in pairs or smaller groups—and may even have a prayer partner outside of team meetings. Many teams have a *prayer champion* of sorts, who may be a person particularly gifted in intercession or discernment, who helps to guide this process. It is helpful to intentionally structure time for listening to the Lord and sharing what we hear and see from God with one another. Once again, if God is the source of the transformation we want to see, and we want to join Jesus in mission and bear the fruit of the Spirit to the glory of God, then prayer must be an integrated part of our lives, both as spiritual leaders and as organic teams.

ACKNOWLEDGMENTS

This book is yours, God, and you alone deserve all the glory. Thank you for working in and through my life, for calling me your own, and for continuing to move in your church.

This project would not have been possible without my amazing family. MyLinda, your support and encouragement prompted this book in the first place, and without it I would likely not have persevered to the end. It is my greatest joy to share this life with you, and so much of my own growth as a leader and learning about leadership is due to your influence. You are still my dream, and I love you. And to my kids, Isaiah, Luke, Silas, and Lydia, you are my inspiration. More than any other prayer in my life, I long for you to abide deeply in Jesus' love for you, to share that love with others, and to follow Jesus as your greatest adventure.

To my team with SLI, particularly Craig Robertson and Greg Survant and in memory of Chuck Lord, I am so grateful to have been on this journey with you for more than two decades. I am also grateful for the many other team members and coaches who have been with us along the way. Experimenting together, and being accountable to the paradigm, principles, and practices that are core to SLI, has been quite amazing. I also want to specifically thank Craig for being more of a friend than a colleague during several of my life transitions. In addition to those within SLI, I acknowledge the churches and teams I've had the privilege to walk alongside as a coach. Your faith, courage, and camaraderie in the gospel also inspired me to write this book, as I have witnessed you embodying shared spiritual leadership in action.

I also want to share my gratitude for my friends in the Movement Leaders Collective, and most particularly to Rich Robinson and Alan Hirsch. You have sharpened me and prompted me to more fully and confidently live into the calling I have received.

To my friends and colleagues at Asbury Seminary, I am grateful for the decade I have served with many of you and for the great honor it has been to serve, mentor, and teach others. I want to particularly name my Asbury Institutes team, Shelby Rhea, Dawn, Matt, and Rachel, who became true friends as we innovated and led together. Thank you.

Finally, I want to acknowledge those who helped me in this writing process. Thank you to the 100 Movements Publishing Team. Anna Robinson, you are a rock star. This has been a longer journey than I anticipated, and you have somehow turned me into a writer. Thank you for your patience and gracious support. I also want to particularly thank Ron Crandall, Aaron Buttery, Tod Bolsinger, Jaap Ketelaar, Tara Gazaway, Jorge Acevedo, Carolyn Sims, and David Bales for your friendship and for helping me clarify what to sharpen and what to abandon in order to communicate this message of leading together more clearly.

My life has been a journey of leading together with all of you, and this book would not have been possible without that journey and without the part you have all played in my life. I am grateful to have had so many great mentors, colleagues, friends, and family. Thank you.

NOTES

FOREWORD

[1] See Philippians 2:1–11.

[2] See Luke 22:25–27.

PRELUDE

[1] When leading in challenging times, there is legitimate need to care for those who are suffering and to walk with those having difficulty with transitions. We cannot, however, miss that these challenges also bring with them a season of great opportunity.

[2] John 13:34–35.

[3] Ephesians 4:1–16.

[4] For one example, see "Just 6% of British adults are practising Christians, survey finds," national Secular Society, September 15, 2017, https://www.secularism.org.uk/news/2017/09/just-6-percent-of-british-adults-are-practising-christians-survey-finds.

[5] See ARIS (American Religious Identification Survey) https://commons.trincoll.edu/aris/.

[6] See David Kinnaman, *unChristian: What a Generation Really Thinks about Christianity … and Why It Matters* (Grand Rapids, MI: Baker Books, 2007).

[7] This model of leadership is left over from the dominant paradigm of decades ago often referred to either as "Great Man Theory" or "Charismatic Leadership Theory." See Peter G. Northouse, *Leadership: Theory and Practice* 9th Edition (Thousand Oaks, CA: Sage, 2016), 27–55, 185–220.

[8] See Gary A. Yukl, *Leadership in Organizations* 8th Edition (Upper Saddle River, NJ: Pearson, 2012), 309–321.

[9] We will revisit adaptive challenges and adaptive leadership throughout the book. For more on this subject, see Ronald A. Heifetz, *Leadership Without Easy Answers* (Boston, MA: Harvard University Press, 1998); Ronald A. Heifetz and Martin Linsky, *Leadership on the Line: Staying Alive through the Dangers of Leading* (Boston, MA: Harvard Business School Press, 2002); and Tod Bolsinger, *Canoeing the Mountains: Christian Leadership in Uncharted Territory* (Downers Grove: InterVarsity Press, 2015).

[10] See "A flock of birds pattern in the sky," CGTN, YouTube, December 28, 2018, https://youtu.be/0dskCpuxqtI.

[11]   See "Why Do Starlings Flock in Murmurations?" How to Survive, YouTube, January 5, 2019, https://youtu.be/34jaUM6eqb4.

[12]   Matthew 16:18.

[13]   See https://www.gordonconwell.edu/center-for-global-christianity/christianity-in-global-context/.

[14]   See https://freshexpressionsus.org/; http://thev3movement.org/; http://www.newthing.org/; https://www.forgeamerica.com/

[15]   See https://anglicanchurch.net/; https://anglicanchurch.net/; https://anglican-church.net/; https://newroomnetwork.com/.

[16]   See Alan Hirsch, *The Forgotten Ways* (Grand Rapids, MI: Brazos Press, 2016). Hirsch describes what he refers to as apostolic genius or mDNA (movement DNA) in these six dynamics: Jesus is Lord; Disciple Making; Missional-Incarnational Impulse; Liminality and *Communitas;* APEST Culture; and Organic Systems.

[17]   See https://www.spiritual-leadership.org/.

[18]   See https://asburyseminary.edu/.

1. LEARNING TO LISTEN

[1]   Brent Vaartstra, "Why You Should Learn Jazz By Ear and Not Sheet Music," March 31, 2017, https://www.learnjazzstandards.com/blog/learning-jazz/jazz-advice/learn-jazz-ear-not-sheet-music/.

[2]   Ibid; emphasis mine.

[3]   See Acts 6:1.

[4]   See Acts 2–5.

[5]   See John 16:12–13.

[6]   See Acts 6:3–4.

[7]   See Acts 6:5.

[8]   *The Matrix,* directed by The Wachowskis (1999; Burbank, CA: Warner Bros. Pictures).

[9]   Bruce N. Fisk, "The Frog Prince, the Matrix, and the Way of the Cross," Forum at Westmont College, September 25, 2000.

[10]   Philippians 2:1–4, paraphrased from *The Message.*

[11]   Peter would have been included as one of the Twelve mentioned in Acts 6. Contrast Peter in this scene with his earlier times with Jesus, when he always had to be the one talking! Yet here, Peter doesn't make the decision or try to be the big shot.

[12]   See Hirsch, *The Forgotten Ways.* When Hirsch lists the dynamics of mDNA (movement DNA), he makes it clear that the first—Jesus is Lord—is central.

[13]   See John 15.

[14]   See Galatians 5:22–23.

[15]   The illustration of the medical doctor is drawn from Heifetz, *Leadership Without Easy Answers.*

[16]   See discussion of adaptive challenges in the Prelude.

17 Heifetz and Linsky, *Leadership on the Line,* 13–20.

18 Ibid., 13–20.

19 Ibid., 123–139.

20 Rosamund Stone Zander and Benjamin Zander, *The Art of Possibility: Transforming Professional and Personal Life* (New York: Penguin Books, 2002).

21 See Acts 7.

22 See Acts 8.

23 *Wonder Woman,* directed by Patty Jenkins (2017; Burbank, CA: Warner Bros. Pictures).

24 For a description of the weaknesses of this theory, see Gary Yukl, "An Evaluation of Conceptual Weaknesses in Transformational and Charismatic Leadership Theories," *Leadership Quarterly*, Vol 10, Issue 2 (Summer 1999).

25 See "A Biblical Worldview Has a Radical Effect on a Person's Life," *Barna,* December 3, 2003, https://www.barna.com/research/a-biblical-worldview-has-a-radical-effect-on-a-persons-life/.

26 While I may find it necessary to share leadership because of these challenges, leading and discerning together with others is actually a more fruitful way to lead—even when we are not in a season of challenge.

2. SOLOING AND SUPPORTING

1 *Iron Man 3*, directed by Shane Black (2013; Burbank, CA: Marvel Studios).

2 http://www.egracechurch.com/.

3 Conversation with Jorge Acevedo on May 13, 2021.

4 Conversation with David Bales on April 6, 2021.

5 Frank Barrett, *Yes to the Mess: Surprising Leadership Lessons from Jazz* (Boston, MA: Harvard Business Review Press, 2012).

6 J. R. Woodward and Dan White, Jr., *The Church as Movement: Starting and Sustaining Missional-Incarnational Communities* (Downers Grove, IL: InterVarsity Press, 2016), 56.

7 Ibid., 56.

8 Jene Twenge, *Generation Me: Why Today's Young Americans Are More Confident, Assertive, Entitled—and More Miserable than Ever Before* (New York: Atria Books, 2014).

9 Woodward and White, *The Church as Movement*, 54.

10 Jim Collins, "Level 5 Leadership"; talk at 2003 Willow Creek Association Global Leadership Summit.

11 Patrick Lencioni, *The Advantage: Why Organizational Health Trumps Everything Else in Business* (San Francisco: Jossey-Bass, 2012).

12 Patrick Lencioni, *The Five Dysfunctions of a Team* (San Francisco: Jossey-Bass, 2002).

13 I will use the language of *generative* throughout the book. According to Merriam-Webster, generative is defined as: "having the power or function of generating,

originating, producing, or reproducing (https://www.merriam-webster.com/diction-ary/generative). Particularly, I think of generative as that which gives birth to some-thing that then gives birth to something else. In other words, generative has to do with reproduction of DNA from one generation to another to another to another.

3. THE BEAUTY OF HARMONY

1   See Exodus 18:18 NLT.

2   See Ezra 7:11.

3   See Nehemiah 1.

4   See Matthew 14:13–21.

5   See Matthew 10.

6   See Matthew 28:18–20.

7   For more on APEST, see Alan Hirsch, *The Forgotten Ways*. APEST culture is one of the six dynamics of mDNA. See also Alan Hirsch, *5Q: Reactivating the Original Intelligence and Capacity of the Body of Christ* (Atlanta: 100 Movements Publishing, 2017).

8   For more on the community of the Trinity, see J. R. Woodward's book *Creating a Missional Culture* (Downers Grove, IL: InterVarsity Press, 2012), 88–92.

9   See John 17:20–21.

10   See John 17:11b, 20–23.

11   Note the use of the Greek word "ἀγάπη" (agape) in passages where love is described as the sum of everything, such as Matthew 22:37–40, Galatians 5:14, and James 2:8.

12   See I John 4:7–21. "God is love" is specifically verse 16b.

13   John 17:23, 26.

14   See Michelle L. Buck, "The Power of 'Both-And' Thinking: Embracing Apparent Contradictions Can Enhance Healing," *Psychology Today*, October 22, 2020, https://www.psychologytoday.com/gb/blog/unleashing-the-potential/202010/the-power-both-and-thinking.

15   Alan Hirsch and Mark Nelson, *Reframation: Seeing God, People, and Mission through Reenchanted Frames* (Cody, WY: 100 Movements Publishing, 2019), 135.

16   See Genesis 1:26–31.

17   See passages like Luke 4:42-44; Luke 19:10; and Matthew 28:18-20.

18   This question is part of the process SLI uses to develop a team covenant. See Appendix B on "Creating a Strong Team Covenant" for detailed practices on developing covenant with a team.

19   Organizational scholars have studied different approaches to leadership, and some have named the benefits of utilizing shared leadership. This typically shows up in ref-erence to organizations where teams are often defined as a place where both task and relationships occur simultaneously. When people work in teams, they often experience greater job satisfaction because they are not merely focusing on getting a task done. When rooted in trusting relationships, work is more fulfilling. It certainly takes time to develop these sorts of teams, but the long-term rewards yield both an increase in

generative results and more fulfilled people. See Greg Stewart, Charles Manz, and Henry P. Sims, *Team Work and Group Dynamics* (New York: John Wiley & Sons, Inc., 1999); B. W. Tuckman, "Developmental Sequence in Small Groups," *Psychological Bulletin*, 63 (June 1965): 384–399; and Lencioni, *The Five Dysfunctions of a Team*.

[20]   Woodward and White, *The Church as Movement*, 57–58.

[21]   Hirsch, *The Forgotten Ways*; see the chapter on "Liminality and *Communitas*."

[22]   SLI often refers to these *organic* teams as *operational* teams because their influence and leadership is ongoing.

[23]   Barrett, *Yes to the Mess*.

[24]   See Robert Quinn's book *Change the World* (San Francisco, CA: Jossey-Bass, 2000), where he looks at this by describing Jesus, Gandhi, and Martin Luther King, Jr., as the three most transformational change agents in history.

[25]   See again Lencioni, *The Five Dysfunctions of a Team*.

[26]   "Brian Eno on Genius, and 'Scenius,'" *Synthtopia*, June 9, 2009, https://www.synthtopia.com/content/2009/07/09/brian-eno-on-genius-and-scenius/.

[27]   See John 15:1–11.

4. CHANGED BY THE MUSIC

[1]   See https://www.benjaminzander.org/ for more resources by Benjamin Zander. The performance referenced can be viewed in the Groh Productions film *Leadership: The Art of Possibility*, 2006. See http://www.grohtv.com/products/previews-both.shtml.

[2]   John Wesley, *The Works of John Wesley, 3rd Edition: Wesley's Works Vol. V. Sermon XVI: The Means of Grace* (Grand Rapids: Baker Books, 1978) (reprinted from 1872 edition issued by Wesleyan Methodist Book Room, London), 201 (emphasis mine).

[3]   Wesley emphasized prayer (both private and public), searching the Scriptures, and Holy Communion as a means of grace, which he called *works of piety*. He also emphasized attending to the needs of the least, the last, and the lost—"such as feeding the hungry, clothing the naked, entertaining the stranger, visiting those that are in prison, or sick," which he referred to as *works of mercy*. According to Wesley, both works of piety *and* works of mercy are necessary for sanctification. See Wesley, *Wesley's Works Vol. VI. Sermon XLIII: The Scripture Way of Salvation*, 51.

[4]   See Frank Barrett, *Yes to the Mess*.

[5]   For a helpful look at relationship *with* God, see Skye Jethani, *With: Reimagining the Way You Relate to God* (Nashville, TN: Thomas Nelson, 2011).

[6]   See Exodus 16, particularly verses 15-21.

[7]   Dallas Willard, *The Great Omission*, Kindle edition, Kindle location 567.

[8]   *The Book of Common Prayer* (New York: Church Publishing, 1979).

[9]   Willard, *The Great Omission*, see the section on "Practicing the Presence of God" in chapter 11.

[10]   See 1 John 3:1 and John 15:12–17.

[11]   See John 15:9–11.

12   See the Lord's Prayer in Matthew 6:9–13 and Luke 11:2–4.

13   See Revelation 4:10.

14   See Philippians 3:7–14.

15   Galatians 2:20.

16   See Mihaly Csikszentmihalyi, *Flow: The Psychology of Optimal Experience* (New York: Harper Perennial Modern Classics, 2008).

17   Quinn, *Change the World*, 210.

18   See Acts 1:8.

19   See 2 Corinthians 3:17–18.

20   See Colossians 1:27.

21   See Galatians 5:22–23.

22   See Exodus 33:12–23.

23   See Galatians 5:22–23.

24   I highly recommend Peter Scazzero's *Emotionally Healthy Spirituality: It's Impossible to Be Spiritually Mature, While Remaining Emotionally Immature* (Grand Rapids: Zondervan, 2017).

25   From the hymn *And Can It Be* by Charles Wesley, 1738.

26   See Ephesians 5:1–2.

27   See https://www.spiritual-leadership.org/offerings/.

28   See John 14:14–31; 15:26–16:15.

29   See Galatians 5:22–23.

30   See John 5:30–31.

31   N. T. Wright. *After You Believe: Why Christian Character Matters* (New York: HarperCollins, 2010), 238.

32   For examples of where the Apostle Paul challenges us to "put off" the old and "put on" the new, see Romans 13; 1 Corinthians 15; 2 Corinthians 5; Galatians 5; Ephesians 6; Colossians 3; and 1 Thessalonians 5.

5. DISSONANCE, HARMONY, AND POSSIBILITY

1   Ronald Heifetz, Alexander Grashow, and Martin Linsky, *The Practice of Adaptive Leadership: Tools and Tactics for Changing Your Organization and the World* (Boston: Harvard Business Press, 2009), 150.

2   Ibid., 151.

3   Heifetz and Linsky, *Leadership on the Line,* 13.

4   Ibid., 13.

5   Ibid., 13–14.

6   Edwin F. Friedman, *A Failure of Nerve: Leadership in the Age of the Quick Fix,* 10th *Anniversary Edition* (New York: Church Publishing, 2017).

7   Heifetz & Linsky, *Leadership on the Line*, 14.

8   Robin Hood, directed by Otto Bathurst (2018; Santa Monica, CA: Summit Entertainment).

9   See 2 Corinthians 3:18.

10   Chip Heath and Dan Heath, *Switch: How to Change Things when Change is Hard* (New York: Crown Business, 2010), Kindle edition, Kindle location 90.

11   See Jonathan Haidt, *The Happiness Hypothesis: Finding Modern Truth in Ancient Wisdom* (New York: Basic Books, 2006).

12   Heath & Heath, *Switch*, Kindle edition, Kindle location 90.

13   Ibid., Kindle location 115.

14   Much of this section on an adaptive leadership process is taken from Mary Uhl-Bien, Russ Marion, and Bill McKelvey, "Complexity leadership theory: Shifting leadership from the industrial age to the knowledge era," *Leadership Quarterly*, 18(4), (2007), 298–18. Also see Bryan Sims, *Complexity, Adaptive Leadership, Phase Transition, and New Emergent Order: A Case Study of the Northwest Texas Conference of the United Methodist Church*, doctoral dissertation, Regent University, 2009.

15   For more on liminality, see Victor Turner, *The Ritual Process: Structure and Anti-Structure* (New York: Routledge, 1995) (originally in Lewis Henry Morgan Lecture Series, 1966). Also see Hirsch, *The Forgotten Ways*.

16   See "Strategies for Winter—Webinar, Vimeo video, 1:01, April 30, 2020, https://vimeo.com/413702797.

17   See Hirsch's chapter on "Liminality and *Communitas*" in *The Forgotten Ways*.

18   See Acts 2:42–47.

19   See David Bryant, *Concerts of Prayer: For Spiritual Awakening and World Evangelization* (Grand Rapids, MI: Baker, 1988).

20   This L3 model will be discussed in more detail later in the book. See Spiritual Leadership, Inc. (SLI) website for more on L3 (loving, learning, leading) model http://spiritual-leadership.org/.

21   Remember Acts 15:28 as they discerned what "seemed good to the Holy Spirit and to them."

22   See Ephesians 3:20–21.

23   This process of gaining clarity will be described in more detail in chapter eight.

24   See John 17.

25   See Acts 15:28.

26   These are the six dynamics of mDNA (movement DNA). According to Hirsch, they are necessary for a multiplying movement and represent the originating DNA of the early Church. See Hirsch, *The Forgotten Ways*.

27   See Robert E. Quinn, *Deep Change: Discovering the Leader Within* (San Francisco, CA: Jossey-Bass, 1996).

6. MIMICKING THE MASTER

1   See John 21:1–8.

2   See John 18:15–18.

3   See John 21:9–14.

4   See Matthew 16:21–23.

5   See 1 Peter 1:15–23.

6   See 1 Peter 3:14–18.

7   See 1 Peter 4:7–11.

8   See 1 Peter 5:1–6.

9   See Romans 2:4.

10   See John 21:17.

11   See again the Greek use of "ἀγαπή" (agape) describing "God is love" (1 John 4:8b) and in passages where love is described as the sum of everything, such as Matthew 22:37–40, Galatians 5:14, and James 2:8.

12   See John 21:15–17. Peter uses the Greek word φιλῶ (philô), which is an alternative form of φιλέω (philéō). Then Jesus uses this same word in his third question, and Peter responds with the same.

13   See John 21:15–17.

14   See Matthew 4:18–22, where Jesus called Peter, Andrew, James, and John.

15   See John 15:9–11.

16   See John 21:15–17.

17   See Matthew 4:19.

18   We first see this language as Moses nears the end of his life when he prays to God that the people would not be left "like sheep without a shepherd" (see Numbers 27:17). Joshua is raised up by God to shepherd the people into the Promised Land. David uses the language, most notably in Psalm 23, in which he writes, "The Lord is my shepherd." The prophets utilize this same language as an indictment against the Jewish leaders (see Jeremiah 23:1–4; Ezekiel 34; Zechariah 10:2; 11:15–17). When Jesus appears on the scene, he looks with compassion on the crowds who are harassed and helpless and says again that they are "like sheep without a shepherd" (see Matthew 9:35–36).

19   See John 10:11.

20   See again Philippians 2:5–11.

21   See John 21:18–19.

22   See John 21:20.

23   See Matthew 4:19.

24   See John 1:39.

25   See Dietrich Bonhoeffer, *The Cost of Discipleship* (New York: The MacMillan Company, 1963).

26   See Matthew 14:1–12.

27   See Romans 12:1–2.

28   See again John 15.

29   See John 5:30 and John 8:28.

30   See again John 10.

31   Philippians 2:6–11—the "Kenosis Hymn"—likely predates Paul and may be the oldest Christological reflection in the New Testament. See Joseph A. Fitzmeyer, "The Aramaic Background of Philippians 2:6–11," *Catholic Biblical Quarterly* 50, no. 3 (1988): 470–483. See also George Howard, "Phil. 2:6–11 and the Human Christ," *Catholic Biblical Quarterly* 40, no. 3 (1978): 368–87. See also J. W. McClendon, "Philippians 2:5–11," *Review and Expositor* 88, no. 4 (1991): 439–444.

32   See Philippians 2:6.

33   See Matthew 23:12; Luke 14:11; 18:14; James 4:10.

34   See Isaiah 45:23 and Romans 14:11.

35   Jesus said this would be the case in Acts 1:8.

36   See 1 John 4:18 and 2 Timothy 1:7.

37   See Erwin McManus, *Stand Against the Wind: Awaken the Hero Within* (Nashville: Thomas Nelson, Inc., 2006).

38   See Friedman, *A Failure of Nerve.*

39   For more on leading with both courage and humility, see chapter on "Level 5 Leadership" in Jim Collins, *Good to Great: Why Some Companies Make the Leap and Others Don't* (New York: Harper Collins, 2001). Also see Brené Brown, *Dare to Lead: Brave Work, Tough Conversations, Whole Hearts* (New York: Random House, 2018).

40   See Appendix C "Facilitating Spiritual Growth in Teams" for more detailed practices.

41   See Romans 1:1; 1 Corinthians 1:1; 2 Corinthians 1:1; Galatians 1:1; Ephesians 1:1; and Colossians 1:1.

42   See Philippians 2:22.

43   See Philippians 2:25–30.

44   See Philippians 3:1–17.

45   See Philippians 3:4–6.

46   Philippians 3:7–11.

7. IMPROV AND COLLABORATION

1   See https://jobs.netflix.com/culture/#introduction.

2   Lizzie Benton, "What is Behind The Magic of Netflix Company Culture?" *Liberty Mind*, September 8, 2020, https://libertymind.co.uk/what-is-behind-the-magic-of-netflix-company-culture/.

3   See Nathaniel Smithson, "Google's Organizational Culture & Its Characteristics (An Analysis)," *Panmore Institute*, September 4, 2018, http://panmore.com/google-organizational-culture-characteristics-analy-sis; and Alan Kohll, "How To Build A Positive Company Culture," August

14, 2018, *Forbes*, https://www.forbes.com/sites/alankohll/2018/08/14/how-to-build-a-positive-company-culture/?sh=7ec00fb449b5.

4   See 2 Corinthians 3:16–18.

5   Alan Roxburgh, *Missional Map-Making: Skills for Leading in Times of Transition* (San Francisco: Jossey-Bass, 2009), 169.

6   Scot McKnight and Laura Barringer, *A Church Called Tov: Forming a Goodness Culture that Resists Abuses of Power and Promotes Healing* (Carol Stream: Tyndale Momentum, 2020).

7   Ibid., 184.

8   See 2 Timothy 2:2.

9   For other examples of creating transforming environments, see also how Jesus creates the environment for waiting on the Holy Spirit and anticipation of the power his followers would receive to be his witnesses (Acts 1:4–8). Then the Holy Spirit is poured out and creates the environment for unity amongst the believers, for awe and worship, for devotion, for steadfast prayer, for bold witness, and for continual transformation of people (Acts 2). As a result, we see the early church leaders create the environment for oneness, boldness, great power, great grace, and sharing everything in common (Acts 4). One leader—whom the apostles named Barnabas, meaning "son of encouragement"—also created the environment for generosity (Acts 4:36–37). How did the early church leaders do this? It is clear from Acts 2 and beyond that the Holy Spirit is moving in transformative and powerful ways. In cooperation with the Spirit's work, Paul intentionally formed teams of elders in each place where he planted new mission outposts. He created the environment for those elders to be formed as both disciples and leaders in order to take eventual leadership of the new church. He trusted that only Christ Jesus, through the Holy Spirit, would transform people and communities, but he was intentional about creating the environments in which that could happen.

10   See Acts 11:19–30.

11   See Acts 14:21–23.

12   See Lydia's story in Acts 16:11–15; see Aquila and Priscilla's story in Acts 18.

13   Aquila and Priscilla correct Apollos gracefully in Acts 18-:24–28, which initiated greater transformation for him and more impact in his preaching and ministry.

14   See Paul and his companions' ministry and travels in Acts 16–28.

15   See Acts 16:25–34.

16   Frank Barrett, *Yes to the Mess*.

17   Heifetz and Linsky, *Leadership on the Line*, 102.

18   Heifetz, Linsky, and Grashow, *The Practice of Adaptive Leadership*, 29.

19   Bolsinger, *Canoeing the Mountains*.

20   See Friedman, *A Failure of Nerve*.

21   See the "Productive Zone of Disequilibrium" diagram from Ronald A. Heifetz and Donald Laurie, "Mobilizing Adaptive Work: Beyond Visionary Leadership," in *The*

Leader's Change Handbook, eds. Jay A. Conger, Gretchen M. Spreitzer, and Edward E. Lawler, III (San Francisco: Jossey-Bass, 1998). This can also be found in Heifetz, Linsky, and Grashow, *The Practice of Adaptive Leadership,* 29–31.

22 For a description of how to raise and lower the temperature in the holding environment, see Heifetz, Linsky, and Grashow, *The Practice of Adaptive Leadership,* 159–163.

23 Hirsch, *The Forgotten Ways,* 159–186.

24 See Thomas Floyd, "Denmark's soccer team lived a nightmare at Euro 2020. Together, they found a way to keep going," *The Washington Post,* June 25, 2021, https://www.washingtonpost.com/sports/2021/06/25/denmark-euro-2020-christian-eriksen/.

25 Woodward and White, *The Church as Movement,* 61.

26 See Appendix A "Building Healthy Teams" for practical suggestions on how to build a healthy team.

27 See again section on Types of Teams in chapter three. This suggestion clarifies the purpose of your board as a "directional team," while casting vision for the launch of a new "organic team" to work on the adaptive challenges.

28 See Luke 6:12–13.

29 As one example of diversity in fitting with Ephesians 4, APEST is a model for healthy teams. See Alan Hirsch's *5Q.*

30 For more detailed practices for creating a strong team covenant, see Appendix B.

31 For Biblical examples of these covenants, see Genesis 2:15–25; 9:8–17; 17:1–22; 19:1–9; 20:1–17; 2 Samuel 7; Jeremiah 31:31–34; Ezekiel 36:16–27; 2 Corinthians 3:1–18; Hebrews 8:6–13.

32 Lencioni, *The Five Disfunctions of a Team.*

33 See the Parable of the Talents in Matthew 25:14–30. See also Matthew 10:5–15; 14:13–21; 15:32–39; 18:21–22; Mark 11:1–7; 14:32-42; Luke 5:1–11; 9:1–6; 10:1–12; 10:17–20; 19:28–35; 22:7–13; John 6:1–15; 13:1–20; 13:34–35.

34 See Luke 10:17–20.

35 See the Great Commission in Matthew 28:18–20.

36 For examples, see Acts 14:21–23; 16:1–5; 16:16–40; 17:10–15; 20:17–37.

37 See "Four stages of competence" at https://en.wikipedia.org/wiki/Four_stages_of_competence.

38 Bolsinger, *Canoeing the Mountains,* 167.

39 L3 is the culture created by SLI (www.spiritual-leadership.org) when coaching leaders, teams, and organizations through adaptive change.

40 See Matthew 22:37–40.

41 See again Jesus' prayer in John 17 and Paul's exhortation in Ephesians 4.

42 Ruth Haley Barton, *Strengthening the Soul of Your Leadership* (Downers Grove: InterVarsity Press, 2018), Kindle edition, Kindle location 1757.

8. KNOWING THE STANDARDS AND THE FREEDOM TO IMPROVISE

[1]   "What Is a Jazz Standard?" https://www.jazzstandards.com/overview.definition.htm.

[2]   "Jazz Theory Overview," https://www.jazzstandards.com/theory/overview.htm.

[3]   Bolsinger, *Canoeing the Mountains*, 209.

[4]   See again John 15 and Galatians 5.

[5]   See https://www.jazzstandards.com/theory/overview.htm.

[6]   Heifetz, Linsky, and Grashow, *The Practice of Adaptive Leadership*.

[7]   Heifetz and Linsky, *Leadership on the Line*.

[8]   The terms "observation," interpretation," and "intervention" are borrowed from Heifetz, Linsky, and Grashow, *The Practice of Adaptive Leadership*.

[9]   Tod Bolsinger, *Leadership in a Time of Pandemic: Practicing Resilience* (Downers Grove: Intervarsity Press, 2020), 34.

[10]   Ibid., 33.

[11]   See again Acts 15:28.

[12]   Barrett, *Yes to the Mess*.

[13]   See again Lencioni, *The Five Dysfunctions of a Team*.

[14]   Bolsinger, *Canoeing the Mountains*, 33.

[15]   Throughout the remainder of this section about "getting on the balcony," we will look at three major phases. These three phases of the "balcony" process represent the "from-through-to" process we have already been discussing throughout this book: clarifying current reality (from), clarifying focus (to), then systems and strategies (through).

[16]   Walter Brueggemann, *The Prophetic Imagination* 40th Anniversary, Edition (Minneapolis, MN: Fortress Press, 2018).

[17]   See Ephesians 3:20–21.

[18]   The practices that follow are merely an introduction into the learning and leading on the balcony and the playing field. A seasoned coach with experience creating healthy environments and walking people through these processes may be necessary to take this journey. As stated in the previous chapter, these Learning and Leading practices are always preceded by Loving practices, which not only form people in Christ but also serve to create a healthy team environment. One of SLI's core learning processes is referred to as Mission Action Planning (MAP), which walks through five questions for developing a core identity and the *from-through-to* process. While MAP is an acronym, it is also a metaphor because teams are discerning how to move from their current reality to their vision (destination), as with a map.

[19]   Examples of assessments include Natural Church Development (https://ncdchurch-survey.org/) and Reveal (https://revealforchurch.com/).

[20]   Heifetz, Linsky, and Grashow, *The Practice of Adaptive Leadership*, 77–87.

[21]   See Matthew 5–7.

22 See Matthew 5:21–22, 27–28, 33–34, 38–39, 43–44.

23 Notice that this question and the process to discern around it is directly tied to the adaptive challenge archetype of the gap between espoused values and behavior that was discussed previously in this chapter.

24 Andy Stanley, *Making Vision Stick* (Grand Rapids: Zondervan, 2009).

25 Bolsinger, *Canoeing the Mountains*, 111.

26 See the Great Commission in Matthew 28:18–20.

27 Bolsinger, *Canoeing the Mountains*, 126.

28 For practical tips on experimentation, see David J. Bland and Alex Osterwalder *Testing Business Ideas: A Field Guide for Rapid Experimentation,* (Hoboken, NJ: Wiley, 2019).

29 Notice the use of verbs in a sequence that can be repeated as a system.

30 Tim Brown, "Learn From Failure," IDEO, https://www.designkit.org/mindsets/1.

31 *Meet the Robinsons,* directed by Stephen J. Anderson (2007), Burbank, CA: Walt Disney Studios.

32 Bolsinger, *Canoeing the Mountains*, 213.

33 Warren Berger, *A More Beautiful Question: The Power of Inquiry to Spark Breakthrough Ideas* (New York: Bloomsbury, 2016), 8.

ENCORE

1 See https://www2.deloitte.com/content/dam/insights/us/articles/4522_BPR-CS_JSOTF/DI_BPRCS_JSOTF.pdf; and General Stanley McChrystal with Tantum Collins, David Silverman, and Chris Fussell, *Team of Teams: New Rules of Engagement for a Complex World* (New York: Portfolio/Penguin, 2015).

2 See Thomas Ling, "Starling murmurations: Why do they form and how can I see one?" *Science Focus,* March 19, 2021, https://www.sciencefocus.com/nature/starling-murmurations/.

3 See Ephesians 3:20–21.

APPENDIX A: BUILDING HEALTHY TEAMS

1 See Luke 6:12–13.

2 There are a variety of tools for discovering one's own gifts, perspectives, and strengths. These could include doing an APEST assessment (see https://5qcentral.com/tests/), a StrengthsFinder assessment (see https://www.gallup.com/cliftonstrengths/en/253868/popular-cliftonstrengths-assessment-products.aspx), discovering your Enneagram number (see https://www.enneagraminstitute.com/), taking a personality assessment (for an example see https://www.myersbriggs.org/), or any number of spiritual gifts surveys. The self-awareness that comes from these discoveries highlight not only strengths but also areas where other strengths are needed to complement one another in a team.

APPENDIX C: FACILITATING SPIRITUAL GROWTH IN TEAMS

[1] See again 2 Corinthians 3:17–18.

[2] See again John 15:1–11.

[3] M. Robert Mulholland Jr., *Invitation to a Journey* (Downers Grove, IL: InterVarsity Press, 1993), 15.

[4] See chapter four, Leading as a Means of Grace, for reminders of those instituted means of grace that the church has always emphasized. One of the goals of our spiritual formation is to consistently practice these means of grace, while remembering that only the Holy Spirit transforms us.

[5] As a side note here, many of us (perhaps all) would benefit from getting the help or advice of a counselor, a psychologist, a coach, or a spiritual director. Those relationships, however, are specifically set up for such advice to be given by professionals who are both good listeners and are well trained to respond to crises. I have a coach and a spiritual director myself for these reasons. When we are coaching, we often recommend this process for those who need it or seek it, and we remind the team that counseling one another or giving advice is outside of how the team should operate.

[6] Examples of a shared devotional pattern or process include Greg Ogden's *Discipleship Essentials* (Downers Grove, IL: InterVarsity Press, Revised and Expanded Edition, 2019), using the Anglican *Book of Common Prayer* (New York: Church Publishing, 1979), and Reuben Job and Norman Shawchuck's *A Guide to Prayer for Ministers and Other Servants* (Nashville, TN: The Upper Room, 1998).

[7] John Wesley, *A Plain Account of Christian Perfection,* 18th Edition (Dublin, Carlton & Phillips, 1854), (Dublin, Carlton & Philips, 1854), 109.

ABOUT THE AUTHOR

Bryan D. Sims

Pioneer, Coach, Writer, Professor

Bryan is a pioneer, coach, writer, and professor. Since 2001 he has worked as a leadership and organizational change coach with Spiritual Leadership, Inc. (SLI), helping leaders, teams, churches, and organizations over extended periods of time to bring spiritual awakening and missional effectiveness. He has coached in Anglican, Methodist, Free Methodist, Wesleyan, Baptist, Presbyterian, and non-denominational settings. In his work with SLI, he also serves in leadership with the Movement Leaders Collective.

Since 2011 Bryan has also been a professor of leadership at Asbury Theological Seminary. His teaching expertise relates to team leadership, equipping, leading change, adaptive spiritual leadership, and the link between leadership and discipleship.

Bryan is a graduate of West Texas A&M University (1998) and Asbury Theological Seminary (MDiv, 2003) and has a PhD in Organizational

Leadership from Regent University (2009). He is author of *Leading Together: The Holy Possibility of Harmony and Synergy in the Face of Change* (100 Movements Publishing, 2022) and has authored a chapter in *Leadership the Wesleyan Way* (Emeth Press, 2016).

He and his wife MyLinda have been happily married since 1997 and have four children, Isaiah, Luke, Silas, and Lydia. They live in Dallas, Texas.

For questions or interest in coaching, reach out to SLI at **www.spiritual-leadership.org**.

To get in touch with Bryan and to find more resources, including articles, videos, and blog posts, feel free to reach out at **www.bryandsims.com**.

Made in United States
North Haven, CT
18 January 2023

31245706R00131